DIVINE
INVITATIONS

The 7 Spiritual Lessons of Relationships

ARDENAY GARNER

Printed in the United States of America.

ISBN: 978-0-578-71338-0

Book cover design: Victoria Lawson
Photo credit: Candace J. Johnston

In loving memory of Isaiah and Sam.

My dearest nephew Isaiah,

Though your life was short-lived, you influenced me significantly. You were my inspiration for discovering my purpose. Everything I am in service to God is because of the promise I made to you before your passing. For your precious young life, I am eternally grateful. I will continue to honor your life and make you smile.

I ❤ U ☺.

Dear Sam,

You never knew how much I admired and respected your courage, strength, and determination to return to a normal existence after the death of your son. You were an amazing woman and mother! My heart ached after learning of your tragic death—I simply could not believe you were gone. May you finally have peace and eternal rest in Heaven with your son, Isaiah!

With Love & Gratitude,

Aunt Dena

ACKNOWLEDGEMENTS

I would like to acknowledge my Heavenly Father as the producer and director of this masterpiece. Without His daily wisdom and guidance, I would not have found meaning in the messiness of my relationships. All glory be to God!

To the love of my life, my husband Fred a.k.a. "King G", thank you for being the leading man in my life and partnering with me on this incredible journey. You are my prayer warrior, confidant, sponsor, encourager, and motivation. I appreciate your unconditional love and support. Being with you gives me the *courage* to be fully who God created me to be.

To my son, Ra'el, you have been my advisor in more ways than I can count. I appreciate your entrepreneurial spirit and drive to pursue life on your own terms. You inspire me. Thank you for listening to my rants about my spirituality, business strategy, and most importantly for referring me to Victoria Lawson.

My daughter, Na'amu, is my master teacher. She is the epitome of strength and has taught me a lot about my relationship with myself. In my revised edition of this book, I will dedicate a chapter to the lesson I learned from her. I am eternally grateful for the meals she prepared and the chores she did so that I could focus on this writing project.

To my bonus children, Shondrea and Shavon, thank you for keeping your dad busy so that I could spend countless hours at the library. It was comforting to know that when I was unavailable, he was spending quality time with you and the grandkids.

I owe my life to my parents, Thomas and Ethel L. Harvey. My father instilled in me at a young age that I could do anything I set my mind to and my mother showed me how "to do it" with grace, peace and love until her transition on July 1, 2019.

Many thanks and appreciation to Nicole Cuffy who served as my writing coach and editor. I shared my story with you and you helped me organize my thoughts chapter by chapter. I am grateful for your patience and expertise.

I want to thank my sister-in-law, Nicole Gibson. You were the first person I entrusted with the completed manuscript. It was hard for me to let it go. You took great care with it and provided thoughtful feedback and suggestions. Your input was a blessing.

Victoria Lawson, you made this book real with your exquisite cover design. I thank you for capturing my vision and making the connection for my future products and services.

My dear friend Candi Patterson, I appreciate your consistent encouragement and support. In my moments of discouragement and doubt, God sent messages through you to remind me not to give up and persevere.

Angel Stanley, thank you for agreeing to be my accountability partner. Near the end of this project, I was at a standstill and I needed someone to hold my hand to cross the finish line. You partnered with me, set daily goals, and we met weekly for several months. Your assistance was immeasurable and I appreciate you for always sending love and light my way.

To all my family and friends that have encouraged me through this process, I thank you and I love you!

Table of Contents

FOREWORD

ArDenay Garner was one of the first people who confirmed my calling for creating videos that can empower fellow Domestic Violence Survivors. It took me years to feel strong enough to own my story and to make it my life's mission to help others with it in this unique way.

So when ArDenay responded to my videos on my YouTube channel and wrote that she was also a DV Survivor who wanted to help others to heal, I was ecstatic. "I'm not alone!" was my first thought.

When we hopped on the phone and shared our stories, ArDenay told me that she recently quit her job so that she can follow her heart and dedicate 100% of her time to our shared mission. I admired her courage to leave a stable career in the midst of COVID-19 to fulfill her calling.

ArDenay sent me a copy of her book in preparation for our on-camera chat, and I was blown away by her honesty as well as her ability to categorize her personal trials and triumphs in a way that can provide tangible tips for any reader.

One of the things I have not done yet as a DV Survivor is forgive my abuser. So I was surprised to see that ArDenay named her abuser 'Forgiveness' and placed it as the first of the seven spiritual lessons I had to learn. The last of the seven steps to practice forgiveness was to trust the process. That's been my mantra for years, and it was great to see that be echoed in this chapter.

My healing journey has led me to cross paths with wonderful people like ArDenay, and hearing their stories help me to know that true forgiveness is possible. When ArDenay asked me to write this foreword, she also let me know that I was the first person to receive the unbounded copy of the final manuscript that she worked on for the past seven years. Knowing that she trusted me with her priceless story allowed me to feel that unspoken bond of sisterhood we develop as DV Survivors. I related so much to many of her experiences documented in this book although our backgrounds and circumstances may have been different. She gifted me with her story so that I can reflect on my own experiences and see where I can continue to grow. And reading her book allowed me to think back on my past relationships as well and salvage the positive lessons I've learned from each of them.

ArDenay and I may live thousands of miles apart, but we are united in our shared dedication to let women know that they are not alone in this journey as Survivors. If you're in the process of rebuilding your life after domestic violence, I hope this book empowers you to embrace the lessons ArDenay shares to live a happier and safer life.

-Christine Lee
On-Air Host | Travel Journalist
President & CEO of Kimbop TV LLC

INTRODUCTION

This book is intended to walk you through my journey of developing a personal relationship with God. The idea of God and the Holy Spirit is based on your own understanding of a supernatural power or universal energy. God represents the source of everything in existence, an external energy that cannot be created or destroyed. Similarly, when I reference the Holy Spirit, I am speaking about the presence of God within, the "I AM" that is referenced in the Holy Bible. The creative energy that implies we are created in the image and likeness of God.

I believe God and the Holy Spirit are one and the same, even though they are referenced separately. For example, I received the title of this book as a download, an inner guidance, from God while taking a shower one evening. In the midst of feeling hot beads of water pounding on my overtired skin, a stream of consciousness poured into my soul: *The 7 Spiritual Lessons of Relationships—you will write a book about your experiences with men and God and the lessons you learned from each.* As I experienced this spiritual enlightenment, an overwhelming feeling of joy and excitement began to emerge within my spirit and I felt connected to a higher power. My inner wisdom was activated and the Holy Spirit began to replay scenes from my past as if I was watching a movie about my life. That moment confirmed what I had been told for years about writing a book about relationships; the Holy Spirit provided a preview of how the process would unfold.

Most often God is referred to as a male and the pronouns of He/Him/His are supposed to imply all of humankind. However, in remaining true to self, I want to recognize both the masculine and feminine energy of God. I acknowledge the Divine masculine energy that aims to provide, protect and guide its offspring in addition to the creative and nurturing essence of God, the feminine energy that commands peace and harmony. For this book, however, I have referenced God in the masculine form for ease of writing.

Divine Invitations: The 7 Spiritual Lessons of Relationships was written for you. My hope is that you will be inspired to seek healing, express compassion, and practice forgiveness. One of the greatest gifts you can give and receive is compassion—the acknowledgement of your humanness without judgment. It's the willingness to see your humanness and the humanness of others and embrace it and send love to it. Compassion is developed through a spiritual eye. I invite you to use this book as a guide to dissect your personal relationships and reevaluate them in order to understand the lessons it was intended to teach. There are seven spiritual lessons you learn from personal relationships: forgiveness, passion, unconditional love, honesty, trust, faith, and courage. Each lesson is discovered through self-examination. These seven spiritual lessons will help you change the way you view pain, hurt and disappointment.

Divine Invitations: The 7 Spiritual Lessons of Relationships will show you how to L.E.A.D. in your relationships when you learn to let go of hurtful memories from the past; express compassion for yourself and others;

awaken your inner creativity and entrepreneurial spirit; and discover lessons in self-betrayal that are counterproductive to the life you desire.

Sometimes we are given Divine assignments for which we lack spiritual understanding. We may ask, "Why me?" or "What makes me a subject matter expert on this topic?" or "Why should I share intimate details about my personal life for the world to examine and critique?" Perhaps you are an aspiring writer, healer, coach, minister, or artist and have been struggling with honoring your gifts, and these questions are at the forefront of your mind about your own work. If that is you, I understand. I asked myself those same questions years before writing the first word of this book. I read numerous author biographies, prayed, and meditated, participated in book writing programs, and journaled about my transformative life experiences with men. In the beginning I desperately wanted external validation that my spiritual lessons were worthy of sharing with others. I wanted to be sure others would value my experiences. Ultimately, I wanted permission. I wanted to be absolutely sure that my purpose for sharing my lessons were aligned with the will of God and not for superficial reasons.

It was not until after I started writing that I discovered the answer to the question of "Why me?" The answer was alarming. I realized that writing this book was not about me at all. It was about obedience, a demonstration of faith and servitude. Do you know that God will use anyone and any medium to bring forth a message to uplift His people? Every human being is called to deliver their specific gift. It is our responsibility to determine what we have been called to deliver, trust the process for the unfolding of the gift, and then deliver our gift to the world.

I am writing this book to encourage women to reevaluate their relationships and reclaim their personal power, and to promote world healing through compassion and forgiveness. I was called to write about, speak about, and to express the spiritual lessons of relationships because of my personal trials of domestic violence, homelessness, abandonment, single parenthood, and low self-esteem. It is my obligation, as a beloved child of God, to share the spiritual lessons I learned to support you on your journey.

The spiritual understanding, I developed from my significant relationships imbued me with an undeniable ability to be compassionate and forgiving. I am constantly seeking, learning, and identifying spiritual lessons embedded in every facet of life; particularly those lessons in which we partner with others to learn and to teach, and to reflect and express our creativity, love, insecurity and fears. This type of agreement is referred to as the "significant relationship." Do you have a similar agreement with a spouse, companion, parent, child, Divine deity, employer or institution?

I want to encourage you to move through your journey of struggle, uncertainty, and survivorship in order to identify your passion, develop your faith, and pursue your calling on your own terms. I once heard a saying that "your pain shall not be in vain;" after you learn the seven spiritual lessons of relationships you will discover that pain can be a prolific teacher.

THE SPIRITUAL PROCESS

In traditional learning, the teacher follows a curriculum and creates a lesson plan. The plan directs our learning and objectives for the class and then we are tested to determine our understanding of the information. The teacher usually gives a quiz, followed by a test, and a final exam. How we do on the final is usually an indicator of our new level of acquired knowledge and understanding. The same was true for the development of the seven spiritual lessons of relationships. The spiritual lessons were developed in hindsight after my relationships ended.

During the relationships, I felt overwhelmed with emotion and responsibility. I was drowning in fear and insecurity, self-doubt, and disappointment. I was preoccupied with surviving—maintaining my sanity to function in daily life. Fortunately, God knew what I needed to survive in the midst of turmoil and He provided. In each relationship, I received a glimmer of hope that my emotional pain was temporary and would eventually connect me with my calling to lead a purpose-driven life. Along my journey, I've identified seven spiritual lessons from my relationships with men and God that have altered my life course. The men whom I partnered with have been renamed according to the spiritual lesson I learned from them. However, not every spiritual lesson was a result of my significant relationships with men. I also learned valuable lessons in a personal development training program.

Forgiveness introduced me to spiritual understanding. He was my first love, the first man I partnered with in an intimate relationship, and he groomed me. Under false pretenses, I gave myself to him and endured ten years of abuse and abandonment that compelled my spiritual growth.

In my dance with *Passion*, my inner creativity was awakened and my entrepreneurial spirit fostered. I learned to identify my heart's yearnings, make decisions based on my own wants and needs, and create experiences to satisfy my desires. I was attuned to my sensuality and creative energy. It helped that *Passion* was a choreographer and exotic dancer.

My union with *Unconditional Love* was an atypical love story directed by the Holy Spirit. This particular man did not meet any of my normal standards for relationships. He was seven years younger and unestablished. It was truly a Divine setup, because after several deep conversations with *Unconditional Love*, I knew he was my soulmate.

I had several relationships with *Honesty*. These lessons were entrenched in self-betrayal and required three gentlemen teachers. The ferocity of self-loathing and disdain increased in my relationships in the aftermath of separating from Unconditional Love. With Unconditional Love, I had finally let my guard down. I was healing from Forgiveness and opening my heart to experience new possibilities, and without warning, my relationship with Unconditional Love ended.

My relationships with *Trust, Faith,* and *Courage* were nurtured through my training at an institute for personal development. This is where I developed a personal relationship with God. Through constant prayer, meditation and journaling I communed with God and allowed Him to take control and guide my footsteps. Here is where the unfolding of the gift began.

Trust was a gift from God. It was a spiritual tool that enhanced my personal growth exponentially. I completed a two-year personal development training program. In this capacity, trust was a matter of allowing myself to submit and be completely vulnerable to a formal process designed to teach me how to embrace my Divine nature. This relationship had the greatest impact on my spirituality by far. I learned to be grateful for every situation, challenge and opportunity, and I adopted a core belief that all problems are spiritual blessings in disguise. This in addition to the program's philosophy that "we are spiritual beings having a human experience" augmented my personal transformation.

My relationship with *Faith* resulted from my significant relationship with my former employer. Prompted by the Holy Spirit, I resigned from my job to start a business as a professional life coach. Through extreme exercise of faith, my connection with God grew stronger as I charted unknown territory.

Courage was the culmination of my maturity with the other six spiritual lessons. It was the Ph.D. course of relationships. My loving partner, whom God ordained specifically for me, presented multiple opportunities for me to demonstrate mastery for each lesson, the most valuable experience being learning how to live life on my own terms, even if I had to do it afraid.

The seven spiritual lessons of relationships are Divine Invitations for you to answer the call that God has placed within your heart to share your unique gifts with others. It is a spiritual journey where you encounter trials and tribulations for personal growth. Undesirable experiences become meaningful learning opportunities and powerful lessons. You develop life skills, coping skills, spiritual tools and resources to supplement your learning. Then you are offered additional experiences to practice the skills learned. After successful integration and mastery of your skills, the spiritual lessons become the principles that govern your life.

PART I

THE INNER CALLING

CHAPTER ONE

"When something bad happens you have three choices. You can either let it define you, let it destroy you, or you can let it strengthen you."
-Unknown

Nearly everything in the beginning of my relationship with Forgiveness was a lie. *Everything.* He lied about his identity, age, children, household composition, vehicle, and his occupation. And he failed to disclose that he had a sexually transmitted disease. I was young and inexperienced. I trusted him. I was open and honest about myself, my family, and my aspirations and yet he did not feel comfortable in his own skin, or maybe, he did not trust that I would accept him as he was. Regardless of his rationale for misleading me, I can't change the past and I may never know why he decided to be dishonest from day one. Oftentimes I wondered, *Why me? What did I do or say to make him think he couldn't be honest?* I felt betrayed and confused because, despite his lies, I desperately wanted to feel loved and to be in a committed relationship. I chose to overlook lie after lie. Now, was I really a victim or was I a willing participant in the dysfunctional relationship?

I could dwell in a state of victim consciousness or choose to find meaning in my relationship with Forgiveness and learn and grow from it. Life is about choices. You choose your feelings, relationships, thoughts and desires. You decide what experience you will have by your interpretation of the experience. The idea that life is what you make it is a powerful testament of your responsibility for creating what you want. In this sense, you are god-like, creating your life experiences with your thoughts. You can think uplifting and encouraging thoughts or you can think destructive thoughts. In either case, it is a choice for which you must take full personal responsibility.

The first choice I made in deciding to be in a relationship with Forgiveness was dropping my standards. I was seventeen, lived in the projects, had just graduated high school, and was probably the only one of my peers still a virgin. I had standards and rules that controlled my relationship with men. My "no five list," as I called it, included: no sex, no children, no drug dealers, no friends of friends or relatives, and no visits to his house. These standards guided my interactions with boys and shielded me from unnecessary drama. During these times, it was easy for me to date one boy one week and a different boy two weeks later because I was not invested in my relationships. In fact, as an adult, I used to say high school dating didn't count.

Practicing abstinence was simple; I believed sex should be a sacred act shared between married folks. I was definitely a romantic. I wanted to be swept off my feet by a knight in shining armor, marry, and live happily ever after. I wanted to experience a Cinderella love affair without the emotional drama my friends experienced after their boyfriends cheated.

Dating men with no children was best practice because I was young. I did not want to be tied to anyone with parental responsibilities because it would limit our time together. I also did not want to bond with children and then be forced to break the bond after I stopped dating their father. This self-loving choice prevented me from having to tolerate or accommodate third parties or baby mamas.

I believed children should be raised by parents who were actively involved in their lives. Absentee fathers are irresponsible, and I did not want to deal with irresponsible men. So if they fathered a child out of wedlock and were not committed to co-parenting in their previous relationship, that was a turnoff. My parents were married and I grew up in a two-parent household and their example influenced my strong-held beliefs.

Ruling out drug dealers was a no brainer. I lived in the projects and my neighborhood was infested with drugs. I had no desire to date or socialize with known dealers. I didn't use drugs or alcohol and I couldn't think of one beneficial reason to comingle with dealers, especially when the nature of their activities could jeopardize my wellbeing. Moreover, we did not have anything in common—the drug dealers I knew did not attend school and were involved in the criminal justice system.

I have always held an unspoken rule to not date an ex-boyfriend of my friend or relative. They were exes for a reason and that was significant. I was proud and didn't want men comparing their shared experiences of me.

My parents, who were born in the 30s and 40s, established the rule about not visiting boys in their homes and I went along with it even though I didn't agree. I thought if my boyfriends were courteous enough to meet my parents, then I should reciprocate and meet theirs. Furthermore, I was "not permitted to have boyfriends," as my mom would say. I had what she termed a 'friend boy,' and he had to visit at my house if I wanted to see him.

Childhood experiences and family dynamics shaped my perception of intimate relationships during my adolescent years. I was raised in a two-parent household and my parents were married before they had children. I was the youngest of four, and my siblings are eleven, sixteen and seventeen years older. In my teen years, I was practically raised as an only child because I was the only one living at home. My family life was stable. We lived in the same apartment for nineteen years. Due to my father's disability, he became my primary caregiver when I was just eight months old while my mom worked full time. Growing up, I experienced very little change. Secretly, however, I longed for change, for something out of the ordinary. Many times I yearned for grandparents—mine were deceased. Both sets of my grandparents died while my parents were young. I wanted the opportunity to spend summers away from home. I wanted something besides the same housing projects I knew all my life; I wanted change. Unbeknownst to me, the change I desperately wanted would come in the most unassuming way. There is great truth to the wise saying: Be careful what you ask for; you just might get it.

For the majority of my life I've been goal-oriented. In my freshman year of high school, I decided my future—I wanted to go to college to get a degree in psychology and go to law school to become a corporate lawyer. At forty, I would marry someone in the military, and we would live happily ever after. That was my original plan—to graduate high school, graduate college, graduate law school, and get married. No twists, turns or hiccups; just a straight, narrow pathway to love, security, and good benefits.

Four years later, I completed my first goal without incident. I graduated high school. In the summer of 1994, two weeks before my freshman orientation at college, I was introduced to Forgiveness. He sent a young boy, who looked thirteen, to ask my name and tell me that Forgiveness liked me. Forgiveness was tall, athletic, and charming. He sported a faded brush cut with deep waves. He was handsome. He seemed more mature than the boys I dated in high school and his interest in me was flattering, especially since I wanted to find my potential husband in college. I wanted to spend my early years building a relationship with a man so that when I turned forty, we could marry. The long-term relationship would allow us to grow together and work through our differences to establish a solid foundation for marriage. While most students were making plans to go to college to pursue an education, I was setting intentions for a long-term, committed relationship.

My need to feel connected and loved superseded my educational goals. I was a daddy's girl and no matter how hard I tried, it felt like I could never please my father. My effort never seemed to be good enough. He complained about how I did chores, talked, dressed, how I did my hair, and a host of other little things that shouldn't have mattered. The underlying reason why I was preoccupied with finding a mate so soon was because I was ultimately seeking my father's acceptance and approval. I was seeking love that I felt I wasn't getting from my father. Forgiveness gave me lots of attention, intimate conversation, and he adored me. He made me feel like a jewel and lost treasure. He said I was rare because I was a virgin and lived with both of my parents.

Ironically, I thought Forgiveness was rare because I never dated or even had conversations with someone of his caliber. We started to hang out more and get to know each other. He confided in me about being adopted, growing up in a dysfunctional family, and his custody battle. He said he was 21 and had full custody of his four-year old son, who lived with him. The more details he shared about his life the more interested I grew in him. He was the first man I met with full custody of his child and the first who had his own apartment. Despite my general rule to not date men with children, I continued to spend time with Forgiveness. He seemed responsible and that was attractive. Besides, what harm could it cause? I did not expect the relationship to progress to anything significant since I was leaving for college in a couple weeks. My expectations, however, could not have been further from the truth. My relationship with Forgiveness advanced rather quickly. I felt mature—I was dating a man with a child; he lived on his own, had a car, was extremely intelligent, and he played intramural football. To some, he was a local celebrity. He was charismatic and many people looked up to him. He quickly became my ideal man.

Forgiveness stimulated me mentally and emotionally. He was enthusiastic about life and the bountiful opportunities ahead of him. He really sold me on his talents and level of self-awareness. He had an organic lifestyle—he used natural herbs and vitamins for medicinal purposes. He was the first person I knew who did not eat pork or beef and he challenged me to eliminate it from my diet.

He challenged my long-held beliefs about dating and relationships. He challenged my views on religion. He challenged my lifestyle—diet, eating habits, exercise regimen, hair products, apparel. We discussed everything, including the sun, Heaven, and Earth, and he commanded my attention with his wisdom. When I wasn't working at my job, I found myself consumed by Forgiveness. Within a month, I was mesmerized by him. Although he thought I was unusual—that is, growing up in a two-parent home in the projects, still a virgin, and drug and alcohol free—he wanted to "challenge" me to become better. Feeling connected and valued because of the quality time we spent together, I welcomed the challenges. In fact, I became so engrossed with Forgiveness that I totally lost sight of my individuality, my standards and my personal goals. All I wanted was more of him—his presence, his conversation, his attention, and his love. I finally felt connected with a man I believed to be my future husband. My wish had come true and I was on my way to eternal bliss with a gorgeous, educated suitor and communicator. I had fallen in love.

Oftentimes, the term "fall in love" is used to describe the uncontrollable emotions and risky behaviors present in the beginning of a relationship. That was true for my experience with Forgiveness. Not only did I fall in love, I lost control of my foundation.

Early Warning Signs

In relationships there are five early warning signs that you are about to experience a lesson in forgiveness and embark on a spiritual journey of self-discovery. The signs include *breaking rules and reducing your standards*. These may be rules you established for yourself or rules established by someone else governing how you conduct yourself in a relationship.

A more obvious sign is when *deception* is involved. Either you tell a lie, you have been lied to, someone has lied on or about you, or you are living a lie. Now, in some instances people will justify lying as a means of protection. For example, a mother, in order to protect her child's relationship with their father, may lie to her child about the depths of physical abuse by the hands of her husband, because, aside from being an abusive husband, he is a great father. Someone else may lie about their biological relationship to a child because they believe it to be in the child's best interest. Others may intentionally lie to be deceptive. When someone experiences a lie in a significant relationship, you can guarantee that individual will have opportunities to learn and practice forgiveness. This is true for the person who tells the lie and the individual that is lied to. Both will have opportunities to practice forgiveness.

Deception can be a disguise for *manipulation* which is the third indicator that one is about to encounter lessons in forgiveness. Manipulation is about power dynamics where someone is taking advantage of another person's vulnerability. It is used to exert control over another person for the purpose of empowering themselves or disempowering someone else.

At seventeen I had high self-esteem. I felt confident in my appearance, my weight, my health, and my hairstyles. I had a small group of close friends. I worked a part-time job. I received good grades in school, did not engage in harmful recreational activities, and I was college bound. I was sure of myself. This would soon change after Forgiveness and I moved in together when I was nineteen. First he started complaining about my clothes and relaxed hair. Then he complained about my friends and didn't want them coming over. He said they were bad influences, probably because many of them knew who he really was. And he coerced me to change my diet. What began as simple challenges when we first met was actually manipulation. Forgiveness could tell that I had been sheltered most of my life. He had a lot of experience, wisdom, and knowledge that I had never been exposed to and I was absorbing it like a sponge. I was naïve and inexperienced and he used that to his advantage.

I often felt discouraged from dressing up or wearing fashionable clothes. I got the impression he wanted me to look worn down and unattractive. I was dissuaded from having conversations with other men because he believed they were only interested in sex. And yet he befriended many women. These were several tactics Forgiveness used to manipulate me on a regular basis to ensure that I would only desire him.

Cheating is another indicator that you are headed for a lesson in forgiveness. It falls in the same category as deception, as it is a betrayal of trust. In the best case scenario, when a person cheats in a relationship they should tell the other party immediately. Rarely is this ever the case. Prolonging the inevitable adds further trauma and emotional wounds for both parties in the relationship. When people are dishonest in relationships it can be likened to stealing—you are taking away a person's right to choose what they are or are not willing to accept. You're making a choice for them.

The fifth indicator or warning sign that you are about to experience a lesson in forgiveness is *ignoring your intuition*. How many times have you said to yourself, *Something told me not to do that*, or, *I knew that was going to happen?* Those gut instincts you feel is your innate ability to sense something without having concrete evidence or conscious reasoning. Ignoring your intuition will most likely produce situations you will regret.

For example, at the last minute your sister invites you to attend a networking event and without thinking about it your gut feeling tells you to accept the invitation and go. So you agree to attend. Twenty minutes before you're supposed to leave home you decline the invitation and stay home to watch Netflix because it was too cold outside and that was your original plan for the evening. The next day you learn that your sister sat at the table with the executive director of a national organization to which you recently applied for a job, and they took selfies together. You missed the opportunity to connect with the director and you are experiencing regret, thinking about all the ways you could have connected and put in a good word for yourself. In a situation like this self-pity and negative self-talk sets in and you are reminded of the many ways you let yourself down, missed opportunities, dislike your current job, and hate the climate you live in. Rest assured this is a precursor for self-forgiveness.

It is important to note how you initiate or contribute to the spiritual lessons you learn in relationships. Consider how you may set yourself up for learning valuable lessons when you break self-commitments, reduce your standards, and ignore your intuition. These unloving acts are certain to introduce you to some form of forgiveness and the lessons will change your inner landscape. With each broken rule, I had an opportunity to walk away from the relationship before I became emotionally invested. My conscious choice to dishonor myself precipitated my relationship with Forgiveness.

Falling in love with Forgiveness was the beginning of the end of my innocence. As an adolescent, I was sheltered by my father's strict rules and mother's protective nature. I did not have free reign over my social life due to certain restrictions. I had a curfew, I hung with select friends that my parents knew and approved, and my dad often chauffeured me to parties. My exposure was limited to the community I resided in and the mall, where I worked. In fact, when I was not working, I was quite bored.

When I met Forgiveness, his two-year-old son was living with him. Based on my rule against dating men with children, I should have immediately told Forgiveness that although I thought he was interesting, I preferred not to get involved with men with children. I was confident and head-strong enough to have that conversation without any guilt or remorse. I was selfish and would not have cared what Forgiveness thought about me or my rules. But I disregarded the rule and made an exception because he said he had full custody of his son. I thought, *How bad can it be to date someone with a child?* After all, there should be minimal interactions with his son's mother, and I didn't foresee any real threats to exploring a relationship. This was the first breakup with my dating rules and standards.

After several conversations, I learned that Forgiveness was related to a boy I dated at the end of my junior year in high school. They were cousins. Forgiveness's father and my ex's father were brothers. This was another red flag. According to my high standards this should have been an instant deal-breaker for me. But surprisingly, it was not. I never had sex with his cousin—we tried to, but for whatever reason we were unsuccessful. After sitting with this new revelation for a few minutes, I explained my previous relationship to Forgiveness. Assuming he held some kind of dating standards, I thought he would become disinterested after learning I dated his first cousin, but to my surprise, he said his father was actually his adoptive father, and my ex was not his real relative. The following week, it was evident that Forgiveness verified my report of my former relationship with his cousin. He mentioned that he spoke to his cousin and confirmed my story and suggested we could move forward. In my eyes, moving forward meant breaking yet another personal dating rule. While the fact that they were not real cousins did not necessarily make me feel any better, I went along with it and continued to be swept off my feet by his advances.

My disregard for my parents' rule of not visiting boys in their home was a true act of defiance. This time around, I was dating a mature man and I wanted to present myself as a young adult. I thought it would ruin our relationship if I couldn't go to his house. Moreover, he was not a boy, he was an adult with his own apartment. He lived in the same apartment complex as me, so it was easy to discreetly visit him without my parents finding out. Furthermore, I had just graduated high school, and would be going away to college and living independently. My parents' rule was absurd and I was too old for it to be enforced.

Though I never voiced my opinion to my parents about this rule, I decided that Forgiveness was worth the risk of receiving punishment. My father was a strict disciplinarian and I seldom willfully disobeyed his rules. But something about Forgiveness made me feel like I had something to prove, which led me to break my ultimate dating rule, established for my safety and protection.

Within three months Forgiveness was referring to me as his "wifey" and I referred to him as my "husband." After I left for college, he was spending every other weekend at my dorm. Our relationship grew stronger. I was in a committed relationship and felt independent. Being away at school meant I was not subjected to my parents' reign and I made my own decisions.

Two weeks before my eighteenth birthday, I had sex with Forgiveness. It was not planned, and I was not prepared. We were in love and my guard was down. I trusted him completely. I had unprotected sex. He said he would "pull out" and that I could not get pregnant the first time. He said his last girlfriend was unable to get pregnant and he was likely "shooting blanks," and I believed him. I did not know what to expect next. As with any exclusive relationship there are expectations and responsibilities for each party and this was something we had not discussed. Our one mutual agreement was that we would only be intimate with each other. My fairytale marriage had just been consummated and I was now in too deep to adhere to any more dating rules—I had given myself to my husband.

Too Good To Be True

Lying is a deliberate attempt to deceive and misrepresent. When lies are told in the beginning of a relationship, the individual committing the fraud has clear intentions to mislead another person. However, when lies are told after a relationship has formed, the intention behind the lie may be a form of protection. In either case, lying is a passive-aggressive form of control and manipulation. When I met Forgiveness, I fell in love with a fantasy. Everything he told me in the beginning about his identity was a lie. The solid foundation I thought our relationship was built on was quicksand. As each lie was uncovered, I sank deeper and deeper into a pool of forgiveness.

It felt like Forgiveness stole my freedom and innocence. He decided in the beginning that I could not handle his truth and so he chose to lie. When we first met he said he was twenty-one and about four months later just weeks after we had sex, I saw his driver's license fall out of his pocket. I picked it up and noticed his name and birth year was different from what he told me. He claimed he changed his name unofficially because he did not like the name he was given at birth, but it was not on his legal documents. And according to his driver's license, he was twenty-four. Something started to click, I had heard rumors before in high school about his son's mother dating an older man. She called him by another name, which is why I never made the connection before. It all started to make sense. Forgiveness quickly concocted a story about his adoption and why the year on his license was different. I knew he was lying but didn't make a big deal out of it. I thought he was mature for his age anyway, so finding out he was nearly seven years older was not a huge concern.

I knew Forgiveness was raising his four-year old son, but he never mentioned he had a two-year old. One day I was talking to his stepmother and she asked if I had met his other son. He was spending the weekend with them. I had no idea what she was talking about. She went on to explain how Forgiveness and the child's mother didn't get along and so most of the time, she would drop off their son. I asked Forgiveness about this and he said he wasn't sure if the child was actually his and that he had just recently learned about him. This seemed odd because the child was named after him and had his last name, an indication that he'd signed the birth certificate. Again, I let it go. I was madly in love and if I could accept one child, I might as well accept the other. As his wifey, that's what I was supposed to do, right?

In my teenage years I was an introvert; I stayed in my head monitoring my thoughts. For some strange reason I became fixated in the 90s on dating a man who drove a Chevrolet Corsica. Maybe it was because I liked the look of the vehicle or I just wanted to ride in it. Either way, my wish was granted. Forgiveness drove a Corsica that he claimed as his own.

One morning after spending the night with Forgiveness at a hotel, his stepmother called my mother looking for him. She said he borrowed her car the night before and he hadn't returned—she needed it to get to work. When my mother questioned me about it, I told her I hadn't seen him since he'd dropped me off. Yes, I told a small lie to protect my life. I did not see a need to confront Forgiveness about this incident because he had access to the vehicle and that was all that mattered to me.

Another major lie pertained to his occupation. Forgiveness said he was a full-time student attending a local university. He said his dad's veteran's benefits were paying his tuition and that he would transfer to the college I was attending in the spring semester. I thought that was a beautiful demonstration of love. He was willing to uproot himself and transfer schools so we could be on the same campus and spend time together in between classes and on the weekends. This would save him money from traveling every weekend to visit me. I thought I had hit the jackpot. He transferred in the spring and everything was going well until the end of the semester. Forgiveness was notified that the school would not allow him to return in the fall because he had falsified his transcript. I don't remember the lie he made up about his transcript or why the school said it was altered, but he definitely had not transferred from another university.

Through lies and deception Forgiveness denied me the right to choose whether I wanted to be involved with a man who was twenty-four when I was seventeen. He assumed I would be more accepting of his four-year-old than the two-year-old. He must have thought it was more appealing to say he lived alone, instead of saying his father and step-mother lived with him, and that he drove a vehicle he didn't own.

Throughout the course of my ten-year, tumultuous relationship, Forgiveness continued to lie about his family of origin, his business acquaintances, and miscellaneous details about his life. I was physically, verbally and emotionally abused. At the ten-year mark I decided I had had enough. I was suffocating from being controlled and manipulated and I wanted out. In 2004, after we returned from a family trip to Disney World, I called Forgiveness from a pay phone at work and told him the relationship was over. He took it better than I had expected.

He said, "I am not going to be a part time father, so if you want to break up our family that's on you."

I told him, "I'm okay with that."

He abandoned his children for several years. When we separated, they were eight and six; he may have seen them once in their early teens. Fortunately, they were able to spend their primary years with him and get a solid foundation. By the grace of God, they were protected from his unloving ways. They had a different experience of him. They loved their father. As parents, we were partners; we were on one team when it came to teaching them about their heritage, exposing them to aboriginal cultures and language, rearing them in a village-like community, and providing them with a natural and organic lifestyle at a time when it was less common amongst our peers.

Forgiveness was a good father to our children. He wanted them to know about traditions and religions at an early age. And I supported that. We didn't let them celebrate Halloween, or let them believe in Santa Claus, the Easter Bunny, or the Tooth Fairy. We taught them the importance of reading and education. We introduced them to the Nuwaupic language. We intentionally made it our mission to build their sense of self from the moment they were born. Since I was the first woman with whom Forgiveness was still in a relationship at the time of his child's birth, he was actively involved. He wanted to deliver our son at home. He wanted to be the first person our son saw as he made his debut into the world. Not aware of the risks associated with my pregnancy and at home deliveries, I agreed. I figured Forgiveness knew what he was doing because he had read a few books and researched how to deliver babies at home.

When my water broke, Forgiveness was prepared with medical scissors, boiling water, and a white receiving blanket he'd made. We tried unsuccessfully for hours to deliver at home. But the pain increased and I requested an ambulance. It was a good thing we did go to the hospital because my son became distressed in the womb and it took another seven hours for me to deliver him naturally. There were complications—my water didn't fully break and I was only three centimeters dilated and needed to be induced to get to ten. My blood pressure had skyrocketed and I needed medication to bring it down, or risk having a seizure. My vaginal walls tore as I was delivering and stitches were required. Not to mention that I did not know how to push, so the coaching by the medical staff was instrumental in helping me deliver and stay calm. As I write about my experience, I realize God spared me and my son. One of us, if not both of us, could have died if I had not gone to the hospital. Even when I didn't know it, I was in the favor of God. Forgiveness had good intentions when it came to our children. He loved them the best way he knew how at the time.

I believe Forgiveness loved me to the best of his ability. However, he had unresolved issues from his childhood that impacted his relationship with me. Due to the nature of his allegations, I will not go in to detail, but if his claims are true, they may explain his inability to trust and develop a real intimate relationship. He was experiencing the ultimate pain and suffering as both victim and perpetrator. Every time he was enraged or yelling, I could see the scared little boy within begging and pleading to be heard, loved, and accepted. Unfortunately, I was not spiritually attuned to provide what he needed or to encourage his healing. I simply mirrored his pain and desires for love and attention.

The Spiritual Lesson of Forgiveness

Forgiveness taught me how to view the world through a spiritual lens with the understanding that hurt people hurt people. Underneath a person's anger is usually hurt, suppressed feelings, and unacknowledged emotions. These situations call for empathy. People want their feelings validated. They want to be acknowledged and they want to know that you see and hear them and their pain. Most of the time people just want to be understood.

By doing my own inner work, I was able to forgive him for the abuse, abandonment, manipulation and lies. Marianne Williamson's book, *A Return to Love: Reflections on the Principles of a Course in Miracles*, introduced me to the concept of forgiveness. That's when I knew that the sole purpose of my relationship with Forgiveness was to teach me forgiveness. He was undoubtedly a master teacher.

Seven Steps to Practice Forgiveness

1. Identify the person(s), situation(s) or event(s) that have caused you disharmony.

2. Acknowledge your hurtful feelings connected to the experience.

3. Honor yourself by accepting that you did the best you could with the knowledge, skills and resources you had at the time. There is no reason to punish yourself any longer. If you could have done it differently, you would have.

4. Write self-forgiveness statements to initiate your healing process. You can choose from the following sentence starters "*I forgive myself for...*" or "*I accept myself for...*" or "*I appreciate myself for...*" Ultimately you will want to use all three to experience the deepest level of compassion.

5. Let go of your hurtful memories from the past. You can't control what happened in the past, but you have absolute control of how you respond to what happened.

6. Express compassion for others. In the beginning it may be difficult for you to have compassion for someone who hurt you. But when you begin to express compassion for people in general, you will develop the spiritual fortitude to express more compassion for all.

7. Be loving, kind and gentle with yourself during your healing process and remember that it is a PROCESS. Do not expect to complete all the steps quickly. Healing takes time. Don't rush the process, TRUST the process!

CHAPTER TWO

"Honor your passion and commit to action."
-ArDenay Garner

The timeless cliché, *Life is what you make it*, has significant meaning for those who choose to create the life they want. Humans are emotional creatures. We were given the ability to experience an array of emotions such as love, joy, hate, and anger. It is your interpretation of these feelings that determine your quality of life.

Passion is an emotion or energy fueled by great enthusiasm and interest and it is often seen in a positive light. On the other hand, rage, a brother to passion, carries the same emotional intensity and is viewed negatively. Both passion and rage are forms of energy that, when directed, can either create or destroy, depending on one's intent. The choice to encourage life or death not only rests on your power of speaking but is contingent on your thinking and interpretation of each event.

Feelings of passion and rage can be a catalyst for people to discover their calling, their purpose, or a greater reason for living that benefits something outside the self. Consider the meaning of purpose to be *a series of natural occurrences that produce change or development.* Within these changes, developments and processes are often occurring simultaneously to create the catalyst for experiencing a Divine Invitation. If you take the time to: a) slow down, b) monitor your thoughts, c) reflect on your past experiences, d) appreciate the present, and e) plan for your future, you may soon discover that all your life experiences, the good and the so-called bad, have positively shaped who you are.

The passing of my 17-month young great-nephew, Isaiah, produced a change in my mindset. I recall holding his small, fragile, lifeless body in my arms and declaring that his death would not be in vain. In that moment, without knowing it, I had committed myself to a lifetime of ministry and social work. I vowed to make a difference in the lives of parents, and in the lives of people convicted of crimes against children. I developed compassion and sensitivity for human suffering. I found purpose in this tragedy. I believed God chose my great-nephew to bring healing, restoration and compassion to the world. I adopted a new lease on life and felt charged with a mission to fulfill my destiny in service to humanity.

The incarceration of my nephew induced my own spiritual understanding of compassion and human suffering. My nephew adored his son. I can't imagine the pain he feels. He lost his first-born child. He never had the opportunity to say goodbye. He was deemed responsible for his death and served thirteen years in prison with very few visits from his family and friends. This is the epitome of human suffering— when an individual is perceived as the perpetrator and victim. This kind of suffering evokes a Divine Invitation.

During my journey of soul searching, I experienced many spiritual life lessons. Each lesson helped to raise my awareness of hurt and joy. In the beginning I sought answers and meaning to my experiences. Losing Isaiah was my first Divine Invitation. I desperately wanted to understand why my great-nephew's life wasn't spared. Why did he have to die young? Why did he leave this earth before he had a chance to live and explore and get to know his family? In searching for answers, I discerned a voice, a small, quiet voice, whispering in my head. It was unlike any voice I'd ever heard before. Each word was pronounced clearly with authority. It was as if someone was in the room with me, leaning on my shoulder and speaking directly in my ear. It was the Holy Spirit speaking to me: *Isaiah completed his purpose and was called home because there is nothing left for him to do here. He was fortunate to fulfill his purpose in a short time, whereas it takes most people decades to do what he came to do. Now it is up to you to find your purpose and honor it.* And then the voice disappeared as quickly as it came and the room was silent. I quickly found pen and paper to write down the message I had just heard for future reference.

A Divine Invitation is presented when God gives you the opportunity to transform your pain and suffering into compassion and meaningful work that promotes healing. You can tolerate the normal trials and tribulations you face in life until pain is inflicted and you feel tested—you may lose hope in the future, become physically weak, lose confidence in yourself, or perhaps you even lose faith in your higher power.

I often wondered why "love" hurt me, abused me, and abandoned me. I acknowledged the pain, the losses, the hurts and disappointments and I gave voice to them. I began sharing my experiences of domestic violence, homelessness, single parenthood, and feelings of unworthiness with anyone who would listen. I attended personal development trainings and workshops, started a women's empowerment group, and volunteered in the community. Each activity provided healing and personal growth. My primary life lesson at the time was to learn and practice unconditional love and acceptance for myself and others.

God can use any situation to encourage you to answer His call. If you are struggling with a crisis or have recently experienced a loss, take a moment to intentionally make meaning out of the senseless to promote healing and reconciliation. It may take several attempts, but you are worth it. Healing is contagious. When you heal, those in your sphere of influence begin to heal and there is no limit to the number of lives that can be restored, recovered, redirected or impacted by your new found purpose for living.

Take a moment to pause and determine your life's purpose. You may identify one purpose or several purposes. There are no restrictions. Declare your purpose publicly by speaking about it with a friend, posting it on social media or announcing it in a room full of people. This act, whether spoken or written, symbolizes your acknowledgement of your purpose. Like a confession, once you make it known what you are here to do on this planet, the Holy Spirit will begin to support you. You will meet new people who can help you along your path. They will have influence and power to open doors that were once closed to you. You will receive unexpected resources that will change your situation instantly. You will receive unexpected blessings that will improve your quality of life and ability to fulfill your destiny.

The Unveiling of Passion

God can use any situation to awaken your gifts from the Holy Spirit. It can be a personal experience, a characterization from your favorite movie, a story from the national news, or an encounter with a stranger at a club. My awakening was sparked by the latter.

In celebration of being single and free from the bondage of a ten-year, abusive relationship, I decided to visit some friends in Atlanta for my twenty-eighth birthday. They took me to a nightclub twenty minutes outside of Atlanta, to see a male revue show. After many hours of searching for the perfect outfit and doing our hair and makeup we reached our destination. The ambiance was enticing—dim lights, scented candles, and the sounds of R&B music playing in the background overshadowed by laughter and chatter that filled the showroom as women gathered around the stage in anticipation of the renowned Black Chippendales.

This was a new experience for me—I'd been a live-in girlfriend and mother since I was nineteen, and though I'd lived in Atlanta in my early twenties, I never got to experience its nightlife. I had a preconceived notion that Chippendales were glorified strippers who should be ashamed of themselves. I considered them morally corrupt and wondered if I was just as bad by watching the show. Was I overanalyzing the situation? Absolutely.

My thinking was rigid. For most of my life I was sheltered by strict parents and then an overbearing and manipulative man who'd held strong convictions about many things. As the time passed, I began to calm my mind and enjoy the evening for what it was—live entertainment.

Mesmerized by the twenty talented Chippendales of mahogany, caramel, and vanilla hues, I couldn't control myself. The performances were worth every dollar bill cheerfully deposited into their mouths and hands. Unfortunately, the state of Georgia had a no-touch policy and I had to refrain from touching the performers. By the end of the evening my opinions of exotic dancers changed—I saw them as gifted artists. They were creative and captivating. Entertaining and well-rehearsed. Most were excellent dancers with acrobatic skills. During their performance, I discovered an appreciation for the performing arts. Each performer was talented. They exemplified perfection for their craft. They were passionate! I was unaware that a male revue show would facilitate my introductory course in passion.

After the show I felt invigorated. I noticed the Chippendale from Alabama on the dance floor. He seemed different from the others. His performance was sheer artistry. He charmed the audience with a choreographed piece to *Imagine That*—I have never viewed pound cake, strawberries and whipped cream the same way. Almost to the point of obsession, I watched him on the dance floor and noticed every little detail. I could see the beads of sweat running down his forehead and milk chocolate face, his sparkling white teeth reflected from the spotlight that beamed on him. He was wearing a sage-colored velour sweat suit. He was battling another dancer. Jokingly, I said to my friend, Melissa, "I want to dance with him." The music was loud and she strained to hear me, so I repeated myself. I had to yell at the top of my lungs for her to hear me. She nodded in response and I continued to sway to the music.

In my peripheral vision, I could see Melissa walking toward Mr. Chippendale. I didn't think anything of it until I saw her lean in toward him, as if she were talking in his ear, and then she pointed in my direction. They both looked toward me and I pretended not to see them. All the while, I was thinking she better not tell him what I said. He was a professional dancer and my one or two steps would look awkward with him. They parted and Melissa returned without mentioning anything about her exchange and I didn't bother to ask.

Out of nowhere, I felt a tug on my right shoulder, I turned around, looked up and it was Mr. Chippendale, he was gesturing for me to dance with him. I paused, took a deep breath, and thought, this is really happening.

In the blink of an eye I was dancing with Passion. He was 6'2", dark and handsome, athletic, about one-hundred-ninety-five pounds, with an eight pack and a tattooed chest. He had a charming Southern accent and was quick on his feet. Passion hollered "Yeah!" and embraced me with a hug, and I fell into his chest. He must have been wearing scented body oil because I smelled an alluring musk. He pulled me even closer and I rested on his chest while he led the way.

Though the music playing was upbeat we danced as if it were a slow jam. I felt electrified. In the brief moments of our embrace there was a transfer of energy. Internally, I had experienced an unidentified feeling, something I had not recognized before.

As Passion was whisked away by the other performers, I felt a sense of loss because of our instant chemistry and connection. I was spellbound. If given the chance, I would have gone anywhere with him that night—a total stranger, in an unfamiliar city, at one in the morning. I would have traveled to the moon and back if he had asked.

A week after my visit to Atlanta, I found myself constantly daydreaming about Passion. It felt like my soul needed to reconnect with him. To address my yearning, I came up with the idea to host a local male revue, a one-man show, and contract his services. I contacted Melissa and discussed the idea. I told her about my ploy to bring Passion to Syracuse in the hopes of experiencing a night of passion with him. Not only was Melissa supportive, but she also knew one of the dancers from the nightclub and volunteered to get Passion's contact information.

Two days passed before I heard anything. Then suddenly, a whirlwind happened. While at work, I received an e-mail from Melissa with Passion's phone number, a link to his webpage and e-mail address. I was nervous and excited and completely distracted from work. I became consumed by thoughts of what his contact information represented. And then it hit me. Passion's contact information represented *access*. I was granted access to explore my curiosity about being with another man. Something I had not considered in more than ten years.

Ever since my dance with Passion I desired sex with him. This desire was far out of character for me and I desperately needed to talk with him to understand the driving force behind my craving. After fifteen minutes of daydreaming and contemplation it was time to make the call. I had to make the call then, while at work, or I would not have been able to focus for the remainder of the day.

I imagined different scenarios that could play out during our initial conversation and thoughts of doubt crept into my subconscious. Would he remember our dance? Would he be willing to travel to Syracuse? Would his fees be beyond my reach? Do I really want to go to this extreme because of an attraction to a total stranger? I ruminated for several minutes and then I called. He answered, in his deep, Southern voice, on the fourth ring. My heart stopped, and I told him I got his number from Melissa, and I wanted to host a show in Syracuse.

He said, "I've been expecting your call. Can I call you back in ten minutes? I'm at work now and need to finish something."

I said, "Of course!"

The ice was broken after speaking with Passion. The mere fact that he was anticipating my call put me at ease. I felt a sense of comfort while speaking with him, as if I'd known him a lifetime. When he returned my call, we discussed my ideas for the show, settled on a date and negotiated his fee. We made a verbal agreement for me to contract his services. The feeling of comfort and familiarity led me to believe there was something more to this newly found partnership with Passion and I sensed he felt the same. I considered him a partner because he volunteered to help me promote my first event. Aside from the idea of a male revue show, I had no other business concept. He thought that was okay and offered to support me in pulling off the event in forty-five days.

During our second business call, Passion and I shared some personal information and learned that we were both members of the same ministry in Atlanta at one point. This discovery explained why I felt spiritually connected to him. We studied doctrine under the same teacher, read some of the same books, and shared similar philosophies about God, religion, spirituality, metaphysics, energy, and oneness. We considered our meeting of the minds to be Divinely inspired, which was the ultimate connection.

Creative Pursuits

Upon meeting Passion, I was entering a new phase in life. During this period the excitement and connection I felt for him was the awakening of my inner spirit and creativity. In less than forty-five days I launched an entertainment business and promoted and hosted my first show. Prior to my encounter with Passion, I never considered hosting events or starting my own business. Without having extensive knowledge or experience in starting a business or event planning, my launching period would have been significantly longer, and it wouldn't have been an easy feat. However, my antennae were up, and my soul was receptive to the download from the Holy Spirit. This was the beginning of a process God would continue to refine until I became conscious of my relationship with Him and the power to activate my inner creativity at will through my business.

The Spiritual Lesson of Passion

The launching of my first business was a spiritual unfolding and Passion was the catalyst. It may have appeared I was going to great lengths to reunite with a man for whom I had an obsessive attraction. But, when viewed with a spiritual lens, something greater, more magnificent, was rousing. I began to discern the inner voice of the Holy Spirit. As time progressed, I noticed a pattern. After speaking with Passion, I experienced an influx of energy and creativity. It felt like I could do anything. If I was discouraged prior to our conversation, I felt encouraged after it. If I did not know how to do something, after we talked, I had an idea of where to find resources. During moments when I contemplated canceling the show, Passion reassured me with specific solutions to my challenges that helped me stay the course.

Our relationship was anything but carnal. God saw fit to use Passion to help me grow spiritually. Initially, I was physically attracted to Passion and God used that attraction to reel me in to develop a closer relationship with Him. Then I made a connection with Passion that made me aware of the power of the universal Law of Attraction, which says, *what you think about and focus intensely on you will manifest.* As if awakened from a deep sleep, I felt revived. I experienced a new sense of self that was sensual and bold. God had my undivided attention because I could finally hear Him as the weight of being comatose was lifted.

My inner fire had been ignited and my very own passion awakened. My inner voice grew loud, and out of nowhere, I would receive random business ideas that included award shows, foundations, workshops, and private schools.

After the third business call with Passion, in what appeared to be a few short minutes I received my business name, business mission, and logo. Seven days later, I registered the business name at the county clerk's office, purchased a cell phone, booked a venue, created marketing materials, and secured two volunteers. The business plans flowed with ease and grace. Every other thought pertained to my new venture. My views on life shifted and ArDenay Innertainment became a living entity. I saw things from the mind of an entrepreneur and each commercial, billboard, and TV show inspired thoughts for my business. My connection with Passion transcended the physical realm to advance my spiritual journey.

Seven Tips to Identify Your Passion

1. Ponder over your life experiences to determine what topics, attitudes or conditions propels you to take action.
2. Determine your personal core values. You can use Google to find activities to support your work in this area.
3. Once you have identified specific areas of interest and your core values, take inventory of the pivotal moments in your life to see if there are any correlations.
4. Write 100 passionate statements beginning with *"I am passionate about..."* Usually the statement(s) that make you cry is what you are most passionate about.
5. Once you've identified your passion(s), explore it. Seek or create opportunities to express your passion through volunteering, community service, leading a project, facilitating a workshop, presenting on a specific topic, advocating for others, starting a movement, or creating a business.
6. Set S.M.A.R.T. goals to help develop your passion.
7. Be kind, gentle and forgiving with yourself and TRUST the process!

CHAPTER THREE

"Each relationship nurtures a strength or weakness within you."
-Mike Murdock

Many people believe there are several types of love: the love you have for your children, parents and other relatives; the love you hold for your spouse and significant others; and the love you share with your friends and community. Society suggests variations of love based on the nature of one's relationship with the subject. Fortunately, God does not base His love for us on our relationship with Him. He loves us without conditions or expectations. For some people that is a foreign concept. Unconditional love is a pure expression of love for which no expectation of reciprocity or response is required. There is no basis for this love other than the need to express itself. Unconditional love is expressing gratitude, appreciation, and acceptance for all life forms on the planet. Unconditional love, for many, is unimaginable. For others, love is an overused term describing personal attachment or deep affection. Some people believe love is a reward that must be earned. Experience has taught me that unconditional love is heart-felt and action-oriented. It is the deliberate practice of forgiveness, acceptance, and spiritual understanding, and it has the power to transform and heal any relationship.

When you experience unconditional love, it is often precipitated by an act of forgiveness. An act that is so moving and telling the response will leave a permanent impression in your heart. My encounter with Unconditional Love was unexpected. He was seven years my junior, living with relatives, and attending community college. He was ambitious, disciplined, and eager about identifying his place in the world at only twenty-one years old.

Two days before my twenty-ninth birthday, I stopped by my friend Karen's house to discuss plans for my birthday. When I arrived, she was talking on the phone with her boyfriend's brother. After greeting me, Karen paused briefly and said she had someone she wanted me to meet.

"He's on the phone," she said.

Intrigued, I told her to ask his age, occupation, and number of children. Karen said he was twenty-one, working on his associate's degree and didn't have any children. I said he sounded decent and it would be a pleasure to meet him. Karen eventually ended the call and joined me in planning for an evening of club hopping and dancing.

The next day, I stopped by Karen's house unannounced and Unconditional Love was there, standing in her kitchen. He was cute. Surprised by her visitor, I felt bashful, yet knew I needed to make a good impression if I wanted to be noticed. As women, we understand the gift of flirting and how it leaves lasting impressions with our male suitors. Unconditional Love and I exchanged small talk about his studies in college. He was interesting so I invited him to join us for my birthday outing. He appreciated the invite but didn't commit. I didn't inquire as to whether he had a girlfriend or not. He knew Karen, so it wasn't like he was going on a date with me. Besides, he was the only male prospect I had for partying with me on my birthday and if that meant he would bring a friend so be it.

My birthday outing was celebratory indeed. Unconditional Love met us at the nightclub, and we danced the night away. I had no idea what a terrific dancer he would turn out to be. Apparently, I have a special affinity for men who can dance. It's something about the gracefulness of their moves and creativity on their feet. It's no coincidence that I danced with Passion on my twenty-eighth birthday and my inner creativity was awakened. Now, Unconditional Love and I had made a connection in the same manner. For several weeks, we continued to meet at the club and dance. Though our meetups were never planned, I wondered if Unconditional Love had hoped to run into me as much as I prayed I would see him at the nightclub.

I wanted to get to know Unconditional Love outside of the club scene. We were meeting at the club regularly. We weren't able to have private or quality conversations because of the crowd and music so I invited him over to my house for Thanksgiving dinner. I was hosting that year and my children knew him as Karen's boyfriend's brother and would consider Unconditional Love to be her guest. Since they liked him, it was easy to extend the invitation.

Dangerously in Love

Unconditional Love arrived about an hour and a half after my other guests because he had dinner with his family first. I was happy to see him and excited that he didn't bring a guest as I had offered him a plus one out of courtesy. Had he brought a date; it would have killed any chances of us getting acquainted.

After dinner, Unconditional Love offered to stay and help me put the food away and straighten up. My children were spending the weekend with their cousins, so I graciously accepted his offer. After we tidied the kitchen, we sat at my dining room table and talked until four in the morning and even then I did not want the conversation to end. Before he left, I asked if he would be interested in having dinner with me some time as token of my appreciation for his help. He thought that was a generous gesture and we made plans to have dinner the following evening.

The next evening, Unconditional Love picked me up and we went to a popular Italian restaurant. We had a great meal and conversation. I was impressed by his confidence and willingness to take charge that evening. When the hostess escorted us to a table, he paused, scanned the area and politely requested a different table. He later shared that something didn't feel right about the first table. He exuded authority in his quick decision to request another table and I felt comfortable spending the evening with him.

After dinner we returned to my house and listened to a CD he wanted me to hear. It featured love songs by Jagged Edge, Beyoncé, and other artists. We slow danced for nearly an hour as I rested my head on his chest, in between gazing into his eyes before our lips slowly met in a kiss. I could tell we were being cautious about kissing. We wanted to ensure there was mutual agreement. The first kiss was gentle and soft; his lips felt like warm butter. With each kiss we became more passionate. Kissing Unconditional Love felt so good I thought I was going to collapse and disintegrate on my living room floor. After what seemed like a three-minute kiss he asked me to listen carefully to the words of the song *Dangerously in Love* by Beyoncé. We listened to the song several times before acknowledging that it would be our song. In our hearts, we were singing to each other. The words in the song were expressive of our feelings for each other and on that night, we realized we were soulmates destined to be together for a reason, a season, or a lifetime.

As time progressed, I found the lyrics to *Dangerously in Love* comforting when I considered the risks associated with letting my guard down and being vulnerable in another committed relationship. We spent the next three months getting to know each other. Every Friday and Saturday he would come over around 9:00 p.m. after my kids went to bed and we'd talk until he left around 4:00 a.m. The time flew by. Not having a TV in my living room made conversation a breeze—we didn't have any distractions. Even my home was set up to help our relationship flourish. I hosted many social events at my house, and it was important for me to have space for friends and family to gather and connect. You may be thinking it isn't uncommon for people to have a formal living room without a TV and a separate family room with one. In my case, I had one living room and TVs were only in the bedrooms. It was a Divine Invitation.

I would never have imagined talking to anyone in my living room for hours over the course of months, especially not a man seven years younger. The details we shared about our personal lives would have taken the average couple about a year to disclose. It takes time to build trust in relationships and yet, our trust was instant. We were not your average couple. It's not to say that we interrogated each other; we didn't. Our souls connected on a higher level, as if we had been waiting for this union, to meet and reconnect. It felt like we knew each other in a previous lifetime. We never had to elaborate on what we shared because we always knew exactly what was meant. Our communication was clear and we understood each other very well. We were both surprised by our level of understanding and acceptance.

When Unconditional Love and I weren't talking, we were listening to music, slow dancing, or writing poetry. Below is the first poem I wrote while we were dating:

Co-Incidence

You light my fire

every time you speak kind words,

do GREAT deeds,

lend a helping hand,

teach me a new dance,

stare into my eyes,

and kiss me until sunrise.

You light my fire

every time you touch my face,

sway my waist,

move with grace,

and flow at your own pace.

You light my fire

I am the candle, you are the wick;

no matter what happens –

we will always fit...

because we are a match made in Heaven.

The concentrated time we spent together felt like we were taking a course in building relationships because our communication was always heartfelt, encouraging, and passionate. We discussed our future, heartbreaks, family dysfunction, deceased loved ones, politics, religion, and spirituality. Unconditional Love was wise beyond his years and extremely attractive because of it. He had a thirst for knowledge, read the entire Bible, was a member of a fraternity, and assisted in the caregiving of his mother until she passed. He was estranged from his father, his brother was incarcerated, and he was raised by an adoptive family of a different race. For a young man, Unconditional Love had had several traumatic and life altering experiences that motivated him.

The difference between my relationship with Unconditional Love and that with Forgiveness was that I fell in love with Forgiveness. I was swept off my feet under false pretenses and manipulation. I didn't have a choice in the matter. Once I learned the truth about his age and children, we had already had sex and I was emotionally attached. However, with Unconditional Love, I made a conscious choice to enter a loving relationship with a man who was just as afraid and vulnerable as I was. I was the first older woman he dated. I was already established—I had a career, kids, house, and I was volunteering in the community. He was just beginning to figure out his future and career goals. He was finishing up his degree with plans to ultimately become a sheriff. He wanted to join the police academy within six months of earning his associates, and if that didn't happen, he would join the Air Force.

He was hesitant about starting a relationship with me because of the many uncertainties regarding his immediate goals. As God would have it, both of us agreed to put our reservations aside and allow our intuition to guide us. When we were together, there was one mind between us and oftentimes we would complete each other's sentences. My connection with Unconditional Love was unique. We had a spiritual connection. And for a young man, he was very attuned to his gifts.

Unconditional Love was clairvoyant—he had the ability to see things before they happened in either a vision or a dream. There were a number of examples he shared about his early childhood experiences of clairvoyance; however, I recall the dream he had when we were dating. One night, we were having a conversation on the phone and he discussed the dream he had had the previous night. He'd dreamt of a woman who was sick and trying to recover. People were trying to heal her, but it wasn't working. She was in an old building near an oil propeller or windmill. The building was raggedy and possibly in another country. He described how the woman died in his dreams and that her death impacted hundreds of thousands of people in the world. He said he saw the number six hundred and a picture of a ring, but he didn't have a clear interpretation of that other than the woman's name sounded like ring because he kept seeing vibrant images of rings. Several weeks later, we learned about the passing of Coretta Scott King and the circumstances surrounding her death.

Unconditional Love used to tell me that one day I would write a book—at the time, it was the furthest thing from my mind. I was working full time, pursuing my bachelor's degree part time, and hosting bi-weekly women empowerment sessions. Writing wasn't a consideration. But he would say it with conviction and certainty like God told him directly that I would write a book. Although I wasn't convinced that I would write a book, I was extremely confident that God ordained our steps so that we would meet and help each other sort through life's dilemmas as two people looking to express love in our unique ways.

Most young men who crossed my path were immature and lived in the moment. They were not concerned about having a career and generating a legacy like Unconditional Love. He was different. Unconditional Love was the only young man that I had a genuine conversation with after I met Forgiveness. If it weren't for Forgiveness's friends, who were much older, I wouldn't have had any conversations with men. Being with Unconditional Love was a new experience. He was a breath of fresh air and I'm not sure if it was partly due to my limited exposure to men, his uniqueness, or a combination of both. One would think that, as the older woman, I would introduce *him* to many new experiences, but it was the opposite. He taught me a lot about spirituality, love, family, and communication. He helped me see the barriers I created to block intimate relationships with men. In my early teens, I created standards to govern my choices about men. After being in an abusive relationship, I created more barriers. These barriers were enormous hurdles men needed to climb to progress in a relationship with me.

I met Unconditional Love in October 2005, about a year after I ended my relationship with Forgiveness. I broke up with Forgiveness on the first of September. For over a year, on the first of the month, I would publicly acknowledge and celebrate being single as a badge of honor and personal accomplishment. Being single meant that I was not in a committed relationship or having sex. I was practicing celibacy so that I would not become emotionally attached to another man that was not my husband.

My expectations for a potential husband required him to adopt my children and give me an engagement ring valued at twenty-five thousand dollars or more. Ideally, if he didn't have cash to pay for it, he needed to have good credit to take out a loan or buy it on credit. The ring became a critical symbol in my relationships with men. If potential suitors did not have the means to buy an expensive diamond, then he couldn't possibly provide for an instant family. I had two children, a mortgage, and car note, and if he could not legally acquire the ring, he was not husband material and we could never move beyond casual dating.

I was straightforward about my celibacy and my expectations: I told men upfront, usually on the first date, that unless we were engaged and he'd bought me an expensive ring, we were not having sex! I wanted men to know I was in control and that I would not be taken advantage of. I was also proud of the fact that I'd only had two sexual partners—my children's father and a one-night stand with Passion. It wasn't difficult for me to remain abstinent. Abstinence was my protection and I treated it like a weapon. As long as I was not having sex, I did not have to worry about emotional attachments or committed relationships, contraception, and unwanted pregnancies. I dated multiple men with no strings attached. I had even been so bold to go to a party once with one man and leave with another because I wasn't ready to leave the party with my date. I enjoyed all the liberties associated with being single and dating.

Another barrier I created in the interest of protecting my children: I did not want my children to meet every Tom, Dick, and Harry I dated, so when men asked about meeting them, I would say, "In a couple years." It was clear that I had no intention of letting anyone meet my children unless we were in a serious relationship. In my state of mind, that rule seemed like common sense, rather than a barrier, and I hoped that other single mothers followed it too. I already felt like I was doing an injustice to my children by not being with their father. I didn't want to set them up for any further hurt and disappointment. It was bad enough that they'd had to adapt to their father's absence. I was determined not to repeat a similar loss with another man. It wasn't worth it to me. I would rather remain single until after my children were in college.

In addition to celibacy and the ring requirement, I continued to wear my engagement ring from Forgiveness. I assumed if a man were genuinely interested, he would take the time to ask my marital status.

Truthfully, I was hurt and angry that I was single and raising two kids and I was acting out. I took my frustration out on innocent men and created barriers as a form of protection and to indirectly lash out at Forgiveness. I wanted men to identify with my pain. I wanted them to feel unworthy, unappreciated, and unloved because that's how I felt. I wanted men to know what it felt like to be manipulated and rejected. Despite how I wanted men to feel, I was never rude or disrespectful. I was friendly and charming because that's my true nature. I simply reverted to my new dating expectations to insult men.

Underneath this barrage of rules and fluff I longed to be in a loving and supportive relationship despite my unwillingness to admit it. Unconditional Love could see through my shield of proudness, strength, and independence. He appealed to my spirit, the loving essence within, and my heart slowly opened to the possibility of a newfound love that was unconditional. We had many conversations about financial security and love. I was adamant about marrying someone that could finance my dreams and invest in my business ideas. I wanted to convince him that ideology was right for me because I tried love once and it consumed ten years of my life with no financial gain. I thought that if I married for money, then at least this time, I could walk away with businesses and assets.

Unconditional Love challenged my rationale for celebrating my singleness. He didn't think it was worthy of praise because he knew I deserved to have a partner—a husband who would love, protect, and provide for me and my children. He suggested I reconsider waiting until my children were grown before having another committed relationship. He believed they could learn a lot from observing me in a healthy loving one. My daughter would learn how to treat men and my son would learn how to treat women. He asked why I felt the need to punish myself because of one bad relationship. He thought my decision to refrain from relationships was the ultimate sacrifice that could have unintended consequences for my children. Maybe they would miss out on seeing how intimate relationships are developed. Maybe they would shy away from developing partnerships with the opposite sex. Maybe they would develop the superman or superwoman syndrome and believe they can do everything on their own because they watched me try to take on the world. Or maybe they wouldn't believe in love and the power of healing and reconciliation. He reminded me that as much as I wanted to shield them from disappointment, learning to recover from it would make them stronger.

You can't avoid pain and rejection; it is a necessary part of life. In many instances pain is the side effect of giving birth to something new, improved, and different. For example, drug-free childbirth is very painful. New legislation is usually passed after tragic events, years of lobbying, and expensive campaigns, funding, time, and effort, all of which involve pain. Children are resilient, and part of their upbringing is showing them how to get back up and start again after life throws them a curve ball. Imagine if your child has never witnessed you overcome an obstacle or a challenge—they would not know what to do when they were faced with adversity at school, in the workplace, or with their family and friends. Unconditional Love helped me see the errors of my thinking and I knew he was right. My children needed to see me function in a healthy and loving relationship and I should not deny myself or them that opportunity just because I was afraid of getting hurt. After all, love heals all wounds, right?

Unconditional Love introduced me to a new love language. This language was complimentary and appreciative. He called me beautiful and thanked me often. He expressed gratitude for our friendship, meals, quality time together, and conversations. He was determined to make me feel like a Queen and was a perfect gentleman. He opened doors and carried heavy bags. He did simple things like wash the dishes after dinner and take out the trash to express his appreciation for the meal. He spoke highly of me to his friends and referred to me and my children as his family. He loved my children too. He took them for walks to the park or to visit my parents, had candid conversations during dinner, did puzzles and played video games, or other activities they suggested. On many occasions they expressed how much they enjoyed his company.

He was a man of many words and my entire family liked him. They enjoyed watching him dance, he could carry a conversation on any subject, and they thought he was very respectful. Whenever he attended family functions with me, he always volunteered to help with set up or to clean up afterward. He met many of my friends and they shared the same sentiments. They noticed how happy I was, and they were happy for me.

Everyone would ask, "When are you two getting married?"

We'd smile and say, "We're working on it."

Introduction to Unconditional Love

There comes a time in your life when you realize God has used a seemingly bad situation to exalt your spiritual growth. After a year of an on and off again relationship with Unconditional Love we reached a climax. The holiday season was upon us and I was convinced that Unconditional Love was planning to propose. It was more than a hunch; I felt it in my spirit. So, the day before Thanksgiving, when we were alone doing our usual routine, listening to slow jams, and gazing into each other's eyes, I told him I had something to share. It was the one secret I had been reluctant to share in all our deep conversations. I knew how secrets created a lack of intimacy in relationships. By withholding information from him, I was ultimately withholding intimacy from myself because I was not giving him the opportunity to accept all of me, including my imperfections. I was acting like Forgiveness, unwilling to share my truth in totality.

After trying to assess his readiness and openness to hearing my news, I finally told him I had herpes. I explained to him that I hadn't had an outbreak in years, I delivered two babies vaginally and they didn't contract it, and since we had only had sex twice and used condoms both times he didn't really have anything to worry about. I apologized profusely. But my words fell on deaf ears. Unconditional Love was crushed. I could see the sadness and hurt in his teary eyes, that look of disappointment after another loved one had failed and violated him once again. I knew the look all too well, because I felt the same way when the doctor first told me I had an STD. I didn't know what to think—Forgiveness was my only partner and I thought he certainly would have told me he had an STD before we had unprotected sex if he loved me. That would have been the respectful thing to do, right? Well, he didn't, so when I told him I had herpes he said, "You probably got it from me," and changed the subject.

But when I told Unconditional Love my status, it was different. I knew I had hurt him and violated his trust. I felt terrible. After he composed himself, he kissed me on the forehead, said "Goodnight beautiful," put on his shoes, grabbed his coat and walked out the side door. It felt like I was watching love walk out the door with no expectation for its return. The next morning my heart was heavy. I didn't know if I would see or hear from Unconditional Love again and I didn't know what to do about it. I was unsure if I should call or text him, or just wait to see if he contacted me. The day was long. I tried to continue with business as usual, but I was too sad. I was sad because I had inflicted pain on another human being, and I did not know how to rectify the situation.

On Thanksgiving Day, I was not in a thankful mood. It was almost 5:30 in the evening and I still hadn't bathed or made any attempts to get dressed for dinner at my brother's house. My kids were patiently waiting with excitement to visit with their cousins, my sister was calling to make sure I was coming, yet I didn't have any interest in getting ready. I managed to throw on some old sweatpants, t-shirt, and a hat so that we could go to my brother's. When we got there, my sister said I looked a "mess." It didn't bother me because I felt even worse. Unconditional Love hadn't contacted me since he'd left two days ago, and I was experiencing withdrawal and guilt. We loved on each other so hard that to go one or two days without speaking was difficult to accept. His positive energy was like having an addiction to sweets—I had to have it.

About an hour had passed, and I was standing at the dining room table when there was a knock at the door. My sister opened it and it was Unconditional Love. He greeted everyone in the living room as he usually did, walked over to me, and said, "Hello beautiful." I wanted to cry tears of joy, but then my family would have known something was wrong. Instead, I smiled while my heart skipped a beat. I asked him how he was doing, and he looked at me with his dark chocolate skin, pearly white teeth and said, "I'm trying!" Our eyes locked and without him saying another word, I knew he had accepted me. I knew he forgave me and I knew he was trying to make this relationship work in spite of his heartbreak. In that moment, I knew what unconditional love sounded like, looked like, and felt like.

The Spiritual Lesson of Unconditional Love

God used Unconditional Love to show me how to love unconditionally, have compassion, and to be forthcoming about my flaws. Prior to my experience with him at my brother's house those traits were merely ideas I'd heard people discuss. I didn't have firsthand experience with it. But God's Divine Invitation made me a witness to its transformative power.

As a result, I shared *love deposits* in my community— these were positive sayings or quotes, printed on business card stock and taped to one-dollar bills. I would give them away at public events. Initially people would be attracted to the money, and then they'd read the positive message. There was one instance where I gave a love deposit to a singer after her beautiful performance at a community center. She happened to be the founder and executive director of her own not-for-profit organization. Through my act of kindness, we developed a business relationship, and she invited me to join a Black educational tour for youth that she was chairing for Upstate New York. For the next three years our partnership prospered. She supported my local Love Campaigns and free community barbecues that I hosted in inner city parks and neighborhoods throughout Syracuse. We provided food, games, activities, and entertainment to residents. We had a volunteer steering committee who donated their time, money, and resources to ensure the events were successful. My friend sponsored the Love Campaigns so that we could solicit donations through her 501(c)3 organization.

I became a community activist and informally changed my name to Nia Love. Nia is the fifth principle of Kwanzaa and it means purpose. The name symbolized my mission to spread love by all means available. I attended numerous community events, volunteered relentlessly, and tithed with my time and money on various projects and programs.

Unconditional Love opened the door for me to experience love in a brand-new way and there was no going back to the old, bitter, and angry woman I used to be. After Unconditional Love joined the Air Force and ended our relationship, I was forever grateful to him for having experienced a love like never before. I knew that if he wasn't my husband, then he had prepared me for him. I expected the next man I partnered with to be even more exceptional, loving, forgiving, accepting, caring, generous, kind, respectful, family-oriented, hard-working, and the closest thing to God in the flesh, and that he would be my husband.

Seven Agreements to Loving Unconditionally

1. I will remember my humanness and express appreciation for who I am.
2. I will remember the humanness of others and express appreciation for who they are.
3. I will actively practice forgiveness for myself and others when I feel injured or cause injury to another.
4. I will remind myself to make a loving choice when conflict is present.
5. I will love others regardless of their choices and actions.
6. I will help someone grow through their experience of pain and discomfort.
7. I will LOVE without conditions!

PART II

THE UNFOLDING OF THE GIFT

Divine Idea

I was created with The Word...

Let there be LIGHT!

And so I awakened from a deep sleep. One of victimization, hopelessness, powerlessness, and mighty defenses.

There was a knock at my door, the doorway of normalcy. "Who is it?" I shouted. No response.

I yelled louder, "WHO IS IT?"

Growing impatient and concerned, I moved closer to the door.

Now in a friendly, neighborly voice, I masked the fear-and asked, "Who is it?"

This time, the silence provoked peace and calming in my spirit. My armor began to disintegrate and the veil of unworthiness and unimportant began to deteriorate into the nothingness from whence it came.

YES!! There it was—that glimmer of light, of hope, of better, of more, of something different that I just couldn't seem to wrap my mind around.

A shift in consciousness had transpired. *What is it?* I wondered. I didn't recognize this feeling. Numbness was my familiar friend of comfort, especially when I danced to the tunes of avoidance.

"Ouch," I screamed. "That hurts!" The pain became unbearable. Tears streamed down my face as if they were in a race; a race to fill my space and baptize me in my own pool of emotion.

Energy in motion, moving through me, stirring up old childhood wounds, past hurts, repressed feelings of abandonment and rejection, and unacknowledged fears.

My soul was ignited. I didn't know...YES, I *did* know; it was the Law of Polarity presenting itself simultaneously as sadness and joy, fear and love, confusion and clarity, and dysfunction and peace.

I AM alive, I declared. *I'M ALIVE! I AM rejoicing, shifting, exploring, and changing for the better. A better experience of this reality I've created.*

I was born of a Divine Idea!

Purposed to be love and share love in service to that which created me.

I am inspired by this Truth...GOD is Love.

I am a reflection of the great I AM that I AM. And I was created in Her image and likeness.

I am a Divine Idea manifested in physical form.

CHAPTER FOUR

"You have to let go of who you were in order to become who you are meant to be."
-Christine Kloser

Relationships have an interesting way of revealing things we need to learn about ourselves. Oftentimes, we project our feelings onto others as if another person can be responsible for our feelings. Many of us have heard a loved one say, *I don't want to hurt your feelings*, as if he had the power or control to do so. The truth is, each human being is responsible for the feelings they choose to feel in the moment. A feeling, as defined in the dictionary, is a general term for a subjective point of view as well as physical sensations. It is also an emotion or emotional perception or attitude. Interestingly, the key element for defining a feeling is ultimately based on a person's perception, which can include historical information; facts and evidence; core beliefs, ideologies and philosophies; personal attitudes; and biological, chemical and environmental sensory feedback. Throughout this chapter I will discuss feelings as they pertain to one's perception or attitude.

Many struggle to express their feelings honestly in relationships. You may believe that if you told your significant other the truth about your feelings of insecurity, he would think less of you. Or that if you told your parents that you're feeling overwhelmed with college and want to take a year off they would persecute you. Or that if you disclosed your homosexuality your family and friends would ostracize you. It only takes one incident of having your feelings invalidated for you to learn that honesty can be painful. If this has been your experience, then you are among the millions of men and women who have learned to mask and protect their feelings at all costs, even if that means sacrificing a loving relationship.

Just why would you sacrifice a loving relationship when it's your human nature to desire loving relationships with others? You want to feel loved and valued. You want to be appreciated and respected. You want loving, committed relationships rooted in trust and acceptance. You want to share your success and happiness with others. You crave these types of relationships because you want intimacy. You want a loving partnership. You want a fairytale romance with the Cinderella ending without taking into consideration Cinderella's struggle. Cinderella was abandoned, mistreated, abused, lied on, and manipulated. Her struggle was real, just like yours. Seldom are you prepared for the unexpected twists and turns, disappointments, growing pains, and losses associated with relationships. Especially those loving relationships you expect to last a lifetime.

Your presupposition is to have high hopes and great expectations for your relationships. Spouses expect their partners to be loving, loyal, and supportive. Parents expect their children to be healthy and grow into responsible adults. Children expect their parents to nurture and protect them, and provide the basic needs of safety and security, food, shelter, and clothing. Siblings expect to foster alliances with each other. These are universal expectations for relationships. What happens when relationships don't meet your expectations? What do you do after you discover your husband, the father of your children, the love of your life, has betrayed you? How do you cope after your child has been diagnosed with a terminal illness? As an adult child, what do you think about the parent whose parental rights were revoked because of their addiction to sex, drugs, or alcohol? What happens to the relationship between siblings when incest is involved? Too often these dilemmas surface in your relationships and you must decide on how to respond in the moment. In these defining moments, you have three choices: you can choose to be a victim of your circumstances, you can choose to be a conqueror, or you can choose to make another choice if your first choice no longer serves you.

Truthfully, there is no right or wrong choice. The choices you make ultimately impact your quality of life. Everyone is entitled to their own feelings, and no one, absolutely no one, can tell you how to feel. One mistake many often make is judging your feelings as right or wrong, bad or good. Whenever you try to intercept your feelings with judgment, you interrupt the flow and suppress them. When you arrest the process, you will eventually turn inward and start self-loathing, negative self-talk, and wallowing in shame and pity.

You must learn how to be with your feelings and experience the feeling through to the end. Feelings provide feedback. Remember, feelings are derived from your emotional state of mind. It would not be uncommon if you felt like you were having a temporary moment of insanity. If you are an exception, then I'll admit there are numerous times when I feel like I'm having temporary moments of insanity throughout the day. When this occurs, I will give my feelings the attention they need. I get still, tune out external noises and distraction or move to a private space, and listen to what my feelings need. Do I need to cry, scream, yell, run, jump, or play loud music? Do I need to talk to someone, write in my journal, or dance? Do I feel like I need to eat? If you can get still, into a meditative state, your feelings will guide you.

Whenever you experience intense feelings, it is usually an indication that you need to release. Think about it: any desire for movement—crying, yelling, screaming, dancing, or performing—is a need to release energy from its current state. Any desire for consumption, such as eating, drinking, or smoking is an attempt to stuff your feelings and avoid them, which is an indication that you need to release. Something is bothering you that you are not ready or willing to address and you try to suppress the feeling by stuffing it to numb it. Any desire to harm or injure yourself or others is certainly a cry for help and a need to release and express what you're feeling inside. Every time that I didn't allow myself to feel my feelings, ugliness happened. Depending on the depth, frequency, and duration of your intense feelings, you may need to seek help from a professional therapist, counselor, or spiritual advisor.

Two months after I completed grad school, I was unemployed, and my house was in the early stages of foreclosure. I felt I had reached rock bottom when I should have been feeling on top of the world. I just earned a degree in my passion field, social work, I was prepared to heal the world and yet, I was not getting any return calls or interviews from job prospects. I was mad at God. How dare God tell me to return to school for a master's and not ensure I had a source of income or employment upon completion of my degree? Oh yeah, it was time God and I had a conversation and I wanted Him to know that I was not pleased with His current provisions for me.

Applying to graduate school was not at the top of my to do list in 2010. I was considering becoming a minister. But after crying out to God for wisdom and guidance, praying and meditating, and listening to the small, still voice within, I followed Divine instructions and applied to grad school. When I was accepted, I was confident God had orchestrated my steps and the next few years would be smooth sailing. After grad school, I needed to make payments on my student loan. I was in a constant state of need; I felt destitute. My faith was wavering. I was forced to cancel all recurring expenses not essential to survival. I lived off credit cards until my account was overdrawn; I pawned jewelry and DVDs so I could give my son a cookout to celebrate his high school graduation; and I babysat to earn a few dollars here and there. I was hustling to put food on my table, gas in my car, and to pay car insurance and my cell phone bill, which were both necessities for acquiring gainful employment.

One afternoon, while submitting job applications online, I received a call from an acquaintance, who is also a pastor. She inquired about my employment status and I shared an earful. I expressed my frustration with finances, lack of job prospects, and disappointment with God. She was listening until I voiced my discontentment with God. Then she decided to give me an earful, quote scripture, preach, and even beg, plead, and cry because she felt I was turning my back on God. She tried to explain to me how it was wrong for me to be mad at God. She wanted me to repent and ask God for forgiveness because she believed that what I was feeling was wrong and blasphemous. She was so triggered by my feelings that at the end of the conversation, I vowed to never speak to her again.

I went from being angry at God to being furious with myself for listening to my friend's foolishness and invalidation of my feelings. My thoughts raced a mile a minute. I was a life coach, I'd completed two years of personal development, I was self-aware, I could identify and process my feelings, and I had a personal relationship with God, yet I allowed this woman to project her feelings onto me. My friend quickly changed the conversation from discussing my well-being to making it about her. Do you have friends like that? They call you and pretend they're interested in how you're doing and feeling, and as soon as you express the honest to goodness truth, they try to make you wrong for feeling the way you do and they cleverly make the call about them by expressing unsolicited advice, thoughts and opinions, and your defenses go up.

I interrupted my process of feeling my feelings all the way through. I did not have the opportunity to make peace with my feelings. I judged them as wrong and bad according to someone else's opinion and I felt worse. When you judge your feelings as wrong or bad, subliminally you are judging yourself as wrong and bad, and that is at the root of your anger. I chose to see myself as a victim during that period of unemployment. It seemed like God had forsaken me and His promises. I chose to acknowledge everything that was going wrong in my life. However, had I completed my process of feeling my feelings without judgment, I would have remembered one thousand times over where God protected, provided, and blessed me. I would have recalled situations where God protected me from danger, such as the time when I got in a car with two strangers whom I brought to my home because they claimed to have found thousands of dollars and they wanted to split it with me, and it was a scam.

I was working as a temporary employee at a major financial institution and I was standing outside during my lunch break when an elderly woman with a man who looked to be in his forties approached me. They said they had found a bag of one-thousand-dollar bills and it was approximately twenty-thousand dollars or more. They needed someone with a bank account to go into the bank and exchange the bills for smaller bills. I was naïve and impressionable because I was seeking a way out of my abusive relationship. I thought maybe this was a blessing in disguise. So I went with them to the bank and waited outside with the elderly woman for nearly fifteen minutes, while the man allegedly went inside the bank to exchange some bills, and then they wanted me to do the same. I told them I didn't have any cash on hand, and they asked if I had money at home. I hesitantly said, "Yes," and they offered to drive me home so I could get the cash. Still oblivious to the scam that was transpiring, I got in the car and we drove to my apartment. I ran upstairs and returned with a pouch of change and one hundred and fourteen dollars in bills. The con artists must have had a change of heart because they drove me back to work and asked if I could get more money the next day. Again, I reluctantly said, "Yes." And they promised to return the next day. Getting in the car with strangers and bringing them to my apartment was foolish and stupid no matter how desperate I was for money. There was no one besides Forgiveness, who was not too fond of me at the time, who would notice if I went missing, because my son was only one and half years old. By the grace of God, I can share this story with you. I could have been kidnapped or even killed, but do you think I recalled this incident when my money was funny?

What about the time when I was pregnant at twenty-one and never, not even once, visited a doctor for prenatal care? For months I lived in denial. I hid my pregnancy from my family, which was easy because they lived in Syracuse and I lived in Atlanta. On December 31, 1997 I was supposed to attend a New Year's Eve party with Forgiveness. I paid one hundred dollars for a ticket and found the perfect dress at Kmart for fifty dollars to compliment my protruding stomach. Although I really couldn't afford to spend that kind of money I wanted to go out and be social. The party was about an hour away from where we lived and it didn't start until 8 p.m. Around 6 p.m., I abruptly changed my mind and decided not to go. Suddenly, I didn't feel like it was a good idea. My gut instincts had kicked in and it was a warning. I asked Forgiveness to sell my ticket and stayed home with my twenty-three-month-old son and ate crab legs.

Later that evening my stomach started cramping. The cramps grew more intense by the hour and I eventually vomited. I think my son sensed something was wrong because he stayed up with me the entire time. At about 3 a.m. my water broke, and Forgiveness was still out. I waited in agony until he returned around 5 a.m. That was one of a few times in an extremely long time that I was happy to see him. We dropped my son off at a friend's house and rushed to the hospital. By the time I arrived I was nine centimeters dilated.

The nurse assigned to me was terribly upset. She was a Black woman in her mid-thirties, and she let me have it. She said that because I did not have prenatal care, I put myself and the baby in jeopardy and the hospital at risk. She was going on and on about liability issues, signing consent forms, birth defects, etcetera. I asked her if I needed a different nurse because I did not want to be chastised while I was in labor. Through the mercy and grace of God, I delivered a healthy seven pounds two ounces baby girl at 7:02 a.m. on New Year's Day. She was a bundle of strength and determination. God protected both of us during my nine months of insanity. My daughter's birth was a defining moment for me. God blessed me with her so that I could understand what strength, determination, and willpower looks like when it grows from a small seed. My daughter is another one of my master teachers in the school of life and I will always be indebted to her for choosing me as a parent.

One time I convinced myself that the only solution to ending my abusive relationship with Forgiveness was to shoot him. Not with the intent to kill, but to make an example out of him. Initially, I was only toying with the idea, until I read a passage in one of my daily devotional books that stated I would have to confront my fear and do the thing I resisted and avoided. It confirmed what actions I needed to take. Knowing that I would go to jail, I made peace with my decision. I believed that I was making the best decision on behalf of all women in my family that experienced domestic violence. I cleaned out my desk drawers and was prepared not to return to work the following day.

My plan was to go to the bank during lunch and withdraw one thousand dollars from my account. After work, I was going to go to a known area for criminal activity, find a group of guys and purchase a gun. After I got the gun, I was going to go home and tell Forgiveness all the things I'd longed to say to him but didn't out of fear he'd beat me, and then I would shoot him in the leg or hip. That was my game plan until I had a Divine intervention. The next morning, my always reliable 1997 Ford Aspire would not start. No warnings, no prior issues, no check engine light, no stalls or delays—the car just would not start and Forgiveness had to take me to work and pick me up, which prevented me from carrying out my plans. By the end of the day, I felt better and no longer desired to wound him.

After discussing this situation with my sister, I realized that had I carried out my plans, jail probably would not have been my biggest risk. If I approached a crowd of young men on a street corner, in high criminal activity area, offering one-thousand dollars to purchase a gun, I could have gotten robbed, assaulted, or even killed. I was not thinking rationally, which is why God protected me yet again. I clearly was not in my right mind. God had to intervene in a mighty way because I had lost it. The morning after my foiled plans, my car started up with no problems. This incident was the defining moment when I realized without a shadow of doubt that God was real. It eliminated any questions I'd ever had about the existence of a force, an entity, or Source greater than mankind. God is real and I'm a living witness to His miraculous power.

It is ironic how conveniently I forgot the times in my life when God provided for me when I was unemployed. In 2010, I resigned from my job of nine years with a major corporation. I wanted to pursue entrepreneurship full time and build my personal development company. It was not easy trying to convert my free services to paid services. Many people valued my personal life coaching and group facilitation as long as there were no fees attached. When I developed a menu of services and charged what I thought were reasonable prices, there was less interest. So quite naturally, as bills became due and expenses increased, I needed to establish a regular income.

At one of my networking events I met a man whom I will call Steve. Steve was tall and brown with a muscular build. As we were leaving the event, Steve mentioned that his friend, Neal, was seeking an administrative assistant for his office and, if I was interested, he would introduce me. He followed through on his promise, and Neal, Steve, and I had lunch at a very nice Italian restaurant. Neal offered me the job on the spot. God did it again! God provided me with that job. I had attended that event on a whim. I met Steve, we walked out together, he discussed his friend's need, and I was offered a job and hired on the spot. My money ran out and my savings were depleted so that job came in Divine timing. I needed a consistent source of income because profiting as an entrepreneur was taking significantly longer than I'd anticipated.

There was another time God provided for me. Over a span of several years paint began to chip and peel off my house. It became so bad that I would only host family gatherings and social events at my home in the winter or after dark. I felt like I had neglected my house and now that it was in despair, I could not afford to repaint it or install vinyl siding. One day, after work, I found a brochure from the local community development division on my doorstep and it had an application for a grant program that provided free windows, doors, and siding for eligible applicants. I asked my neighbors if they received the brochure and application or knew about the program and none of them were aware of it. They said they didn't receive a brochure. Within two weeks of receiving the application on my doorstep, I applied and about five weeks later I was approved for a $25,000 grant to install siding, windows, and doors in my house. To God be the glory!

God has protected me, God has provided for me, and God has also delivered my blessings through others. In some cases, He sent angels to plant seeds of awareness. Back in 1998, I was at the rental office renewing my lease for my apartment in Atlanta. I was sitting in a chair next to the leasing agent and she paused, looked at me, as if she could see through me, and said "I see you're in pain and if you ever need someone to talk to, I'm here." And then she continued processing my application. I neither confirmed nor denied her observation. I simply tried to ignore her comment. I remember thinking, *Well, damn, I'm not doing a good job hiding. Was it my eyes that gave it away? Do I appear sad and weak? Is this woman psychic? How could she possibly know what I'm dealing with, when she doesn't even know me?* In any case, I was not about to open up to a stranger and tell her how lonely, ugly, scared, hurt, and confused I felt. Nope, not me. That would be too embarrassing because I put myself in this situation.

Little did I know, years later I would willingly share my experiences of abandonment, low self-esteem, and abuse with anyone who would listen. I found healing in sharing my experiences with others. I didn't realize the leasing agent had planted a seed that would take root at a later time. When she acknowledged me and my pain something happened inside of me. Something began to stir and awaken on the inside because that was the first time anyone acknowledged the sadness behind my phony smile. For once in my life, I felt validated and I didn't know how to respond. I was not prepared to be discovered or let my secret of abuse out of the bag. Besides, what would she do with that information? I didn't have any family in Atlanta. I was totally dependent on Forgiveness. I was pregnant, unemployed, and had a toddler—how could I make it on my own? Never in my wildest dreams had I imagined being single with two small children, and I didn't believe I could do it on my own.

God must have known that I needed another Divine intervention, so He worked through my friend to bless me. Shawna was married with two children who were not in her custody. Though she was not a native of Atlanta, she fervently claimed the city as her home. On a nice, hot, summer day, we were sitting in our front yard discussing life; the ups and downs and everything in between. I'm pretty sure I was complaining about Forgiveness and feeling restricted because I had two children under the age of three and no vehicle. I felt stuck because I had limited access outside of my neighborhood. Out of the blue, Shawna offered life changing advice.

She said, "You have to practice taking your children on the bus and trains while you're with your friends, so we can help you until you feel comfortable traveling alone."

And so I did.

I purchased a baby carrier for my daughter and pushed my son in the stroller and traveled to Costco with Shawna on the weekends. It took at least forty-five minutes to get to Costco by bus and train. I'm sure there were plenty of grocery stores closer, but we had to factor in my stroller and small children. Traveling by bus and train to Costco was less complicated because I didn't have groceries. However, after I shopped, I needed direct access to the train so I would not have to tote the stroller on the bus while carrying my baby and groceries. My son had what I called the Cadillac stroller. I would tote him and the groceries in the stroller and push it on the train. I didn't buy a lot of groceries at one time, but I managed to get enough to get us through the week, and the miscellaneous items, I purchased at the corner store. Traveling and shopping with young children on public transportation, in an unfamiliar large metropolitan city required strategy and skills.

After a month or so of practicing with Shawna I started to venture out on my own with the kids. Each commute became easier and my confidence developed quickly. It got to the point where I made several trips to Costco a week. I enjoyed shopping and my children enjoyed the outings.

The blessing in Shawna's invaluable advice was that I was slowly learning how to become more independent and less dependent on Forgiveness for our basic needs. I traveled to the grocery store to ensure food was on the table. I was no longer limited to one neighborhood, my children and I attended various events and activities throughout Atlanta and the surrounding area. Eventually I left Forgiveness and moved into my own apartment because I knew I could make it on my own. When God delivered the message that I could make it on my own through Shawna, she didn't just speak it, she showed me how to live outside my limited thinking and small mindedness in what was another defining moment in my life.

You can improve the quality of your life with each choice you make. You must decide whether you are going to remain a victim or search for the lesson or blessing in disguise. Sometimes you can get so wrapped up in your mess that you miss the message that God is trying to give you. As it was in my case, I thought I was broken and deficient, destined for despair because I was twenty-one with two small children under the age of three, in an abusive common-law marriage, isolated from family and friends. I assumed I was destined to suffer in silence because I made a series of irreversible, poor choices. That was faulty thinking on my part and God decided to use Shawna to teach me another way.

Occasionally, God is more direct with his blessings and upfront that you are about to receive a gift from Him because the individual He selects to bless you announces it, and you think, *This is too good to be true.* But then again, when you are the one in whom God is well pleased, blessings and favor flow in abundance.

On a Saturday morning in October, I was attending a mandatory professional development training at work with my colleagues and community members. The training was facilitated in the cafeteria of one the newly renovated schools and I was seated at a table in the front row closest to the presenter. A judge once told me to make sure that I arrive early, stay late, ask lots of questions and sit in front rows whenever I'm attending classes to help foster relationships with the instructors—it could make the difference between an "A" and "A-." He said, good grades do not necessarily come from being the smartest person. Having a positive relationship with your instructor and ensuring they know you can serve you well. His advice stuck with me. On this day, I was blessed beyond measure.

Seated at my table were a few colleagues and a friend of mine, Janice, from a partner agency, whom I had not seen in months. She congratulated me on my recent graduation from grad school and asked what I'd been doing since my newfound freedom from school. We chatted about our new positions and my struggle to recover financially after being unemployed for almost a year. It was a pleasant reunion and good conversation prior to the start of training.

Midway through the morning, Janice passed me a note that read, *Going to Jamaica during President's Day weekend (4-5days). If you want to come let me know. Your room would be taken care of. It would be a simple trip to lay on beach and relax...I would also bless you with a ticket. You are my person to bless in the new year.* Janice is a fervent woman of faith, so I knew she was serious and yet, I was caught off guard by her invitation. We were friends, but we had only known each other for a little over three years. I met her while I was working as an administrative assistant at a not-for-profit agency. Janice moved from California to Syracuse with her teenage daughter to help care for her father. Amid touring the local area, she stopped by our office to inquire about employment opportunities and we made an instant connection. More accurately, it was a Divine setup! We exchanged phone numbers, had lunch dates, fellowshipped, and she volunteered with our program. She was a major help to our program and after I resigned, she became the new administrative assistant.

We didn't visit or communicate as frequently after I became a full-time grad student. I focused on completing my degree and not much else because my internship, assignments, parenting, and coping with a few deaths consumed me. My cup was depleted and there was nothing left for me to give to my friends. I'm grateful that Janice and my other close friends understood and didn't take it personally.

I accepted her offer to go to Jamaica. Janice traveled to Jamaica at least once a year and I was honored for the invitation to join her in February. Janice said all I needed was spending money for food. God is good! In the beginning I was excited for the training because I love learning. After Janice offered me a vacation, I was so ecstatic it was hard to contain my joy and focus for the remainder of the session.

Two months passed and I still hadn't heard anything from Janice. We reconnected on Facebook but hadn't talked since the training and I did not feel comfortable asking about the trip. I figured if she was going to follow through with her plans then she would contact me about arrangements. I knew she had good intentions, but anything could have happened since our conversation in October. Maybe her financial situation had changed, or she couldn't take the time off. Maybe she'd forgotten or had decided she didn't want to bring me with her. I really didn't know why we hadn't discussed the trip and I refused to ask her about it because I did not want it to seem like I was interested in the vacation more than I was interested in rekindling our friendship. Her kind gesture was more than enough to encourage me as I continued to do the will of God and walk in my purpose.

At the end of December Janice called and asked if I was still interested in going to Jamaica. I said, "Of course!" She told me to request vacation for the third week in February because she was booking flights in the next day or so. She didn't have to worry—I had submitted my request in October, two days after the training. I wanted to secure my time off in advance because it is not every day a friend offers to bless you with a trip to Jamaica. One thing was for sure— I was not going to jeopardize my blessings by not ensuring my time-off request was approved in advanced.

Jamaica was incredible. The island was beautiful and the people were friendly. The food was delicious and I ate as much as I wanted. There was nothing more relaxing than sitting by the ocean, eating fresh lobster, and drinking a virgin coconut daiquiri. We stayed in oceanfront condos in Negril. It was the perfect getaway.

The magnificence of God is that He uses every opportunity to bless us. Time and time again, God has protected me from danger, provided job opportunities, and blessed me with amazing friends and vacations. In every situation, I was going through some sort of storm that required me to make a conscious choice to see myself as a victim or conqueror. The choice was not always easy and I'm not saying people are never victims, because that would be a lie. If you have experienced abuse, assault, deception, abandonment, discrimination, or oppression among others, then you most definitely have been a victim. However, that was an experience, and that does not define who you truly are as a child of God. Remember you are the one in whom God is well pleased!

You may be questioning, *If God is so pleased then why does He allow me or my family to experience negative events and abuse? Why does He allow people to suffer? Why does he allow homelessness? Why doesn't He prevent it?* I have pondered the same questions and learned that it is up to us to find the lessons in those unpleasant experiences. When you perceive an experience as bad or negative, you are presented with an opportunity to consider another perspective—one that is more loving and supportive. But this should not be attempted until after you've processed your feelings.

Processing your feelings is an important step in personal and spiritual growth. It aids in the development of inner wisdom, self-esteem, self-awareness, inner peace, and overall positive mental health. Processing your feelings is a skill that requires personal attention to what is happening on the inside. You must be aware of your thoughts. Whether you want to accept it or not, it is true that thoughts create your experiences. What you think about in response to an emotional upset is usually a strong indicator of the type of experience you will have.

When I received word that my 17-month-old great-nephew was pronounced braindead due to injuries allegedly sustained while in his father's care, I knew my family was in for a major heartbreak. There was no way to reverse the tragic events leading up to his small, fragile body being sustained on life support. The only witness to provide details about what occurred was his father. My sister's son fathered the first child in the fourth generation of our family. We were blessed by his life as the youngest member of the family. His smile lit up the room and all eyes were on him as he learned to crawl, walk, run, and dance. He was, by all means, a joy to the family.

We received the devastating news that Isaiah would only be kept on life support until the hospital found a recipient for his vital organs. While Isaiah was fighting for his life, the hospital was searching for recipients, and my nephew was detained. Everything seemed surreal. As I walked down the corridor of the hospital, with family members standing on both sides of the hallway, all I could hear was, *He's not going to make it*. I must have heard it five times before reaching the double doors of the ICU. I probably only walked thirty-five feet from the elevator to ICU, but it felt more like a mile. I had no clue what to expect when I entered Isaiah's room. For a moment, I was afraid to walk in, but I knew I had to lay eyes on him. I had to see firsthand why everyone was convinced he was not going to make it.

I entered Isaiah's private room, pulled the curtains back, and saw his small, frame resting in the pediatric bed. I noticed some swelling on his forehead and a couple of bruises, however, he appeared to be resting peacefully. Aside from the beeping of the monitors, the room was surprisingly peaceful. The lights were dim, and the room was absent of chatter, confusion, and unrest, unlike the horrific hallway production I encountered. When the nurse came in to check the monitors I asked if I could hold Isaiah. She prepped a chair next to his bed and I sat preparing to hold him for the very first time. Unfortunately, this was my first opportunity to meet Isaiah in person. I lived in Atlanta and had only seen pictures and spoken with him on the phone. I'd just moved back to Syracuse two weeks prior.

The nurse ever so gently placed Isaiah in my arms and left the room. We were finally alone. I sat with Isaiah in silence for what seemed like a lifetime, observing every detail about him, trying to find a glimmer of hope or a sign to discredit the doctors' prognosis. My great-nephew was gorgeous, innocent, and fragile. He had so much life ahead of him and I felt my family was giving in too soon by believing the doctor's report. Doctors are not God—they make mistakes and misdiagnoses, and they do not have the final say on whether a person lives or dies. Only God does.

I was in denial and I did not want to accept his death as possibility. I wanted his young mother to exhaust all options before allowing the doctors to declare him braindead. I wanted more time for us to get a second and third opinion. I wanted to enlist prayers and the counsel of clergy. I wanted Isaiah to breathe on his own and show some sign of life. I wanted to purge the guilt I felt for not visiting with Isaiah two days ago, when I'd seen his father. I wanted to wake up from this dreadful nightmare and recreate the events leading up to this moment in time. I wanted spiritual understanding.

After I'd spent some time holding Isaiah, reality set in and I became aware of what was happening—Isaiah was dying. My racing thoughts slowed, and I felt an overwhelming sense of peace and calmness as I acknowledged his precious life in my arms. In this defining moment, I made a conscious choice to search for a lesson or blessing in this heartbreaking situation. I accepted that Isaiah's brief time with us was coming to an end. My mindset shifted and my attitude changed. I started feeling grateful and no longer saw him as a victim. I felt a strong sense of appreciation and admiration for Isaiah. In just 17 short months, Isaiah had done what the average person takes seventy years to do—he had fulfilled his purpose on earth. And it would not be long before God called His angel home for a job well done. I felt honored to spend those final moments with him.

That afternoon, I made a vow to Isaiah: I promised to discover my life's purpose and live it fully to the best of my ability. I promised to become all that God created me to be. I promised that, as long as I lived, his death would not be in vain. I vowed to make him proud of me. God answered my prayer for spiritual understanding after I took time to acknowledge my feelings and process them without judgment. The key to feeling your feelings without judgment is to not interrupt your process. Negative self-talk could have seeped in and said, *Well, why are you hurt when you didn't even know Isaiah?* or, *Who are you to question the doctor's medical opinion?* or, *It's wrong to accuse the family of giving up on Isaiah.* I experienced the temporary feelings of pain, remorse, confusion, and denial and remained in my feelings until I was ready to move on and find the blessing in disguise.

Ultimately, I did not want Isaiah's death to be in vain. I needed to search my soul for a spiritually evolved explanation for his untimely passing. During my brief meditation, God showed me how Isaiah had fulfilled his purpose on earth. Isaiah's purpose in my life was to catapult me in to learning, seeking, and defining my life's purpose to carry out God's will for my life uncompromisingly. My great-nephew paved the way for me to live with purpose and on purpose in service to God and humanity. For his life and the final moments, we shared, I am forever grateful. The passing of Isaiah taught me a valuable lesson on living, and I am a better human being because of him. I am an encourager—I deliberately seek opportunities to encourage everyone I encounter, no matter their circumstances. As long as you have breath, you have an opportunity to make another choice to conquer your circumstances and live a purpose-driven life.

The choice to see yourself as a victim or conqueror is more about your state of mind or attitude than it is about being an actual victim of a destructive or injurious action or agency.

Crimes and accidents occur every minute of the day and people are, without a doubt, victimized. However, you don't have to adopt a victim consciousness and give other people power over your fate. Do not grant abusers, perpetrators, oppressors, thieves, and liars unlimited control over you by harboring unforgiveness. You can choose to conquer the situation by resolving to heal on a spiritual level. Relationships are tools God uses to mold, refine, and shape us in His image and to promote healing within our soul. Their purpose is for individuals to learn and grow through their increased willingness to be vulnerable.

Suppose you get in a relationship to heal or reconcile a false truth about yourself. You know the stories you make up in your head that make you believe you are not loveable, not important, not good enough, or unworthy. The stories you have convinced yourself are true because when you were seven years old you were constantly reprimanded for making mistakes, your feelings were invalidated, or, according to

DIVINE INVITATIONS

your critical mother, you could never do anything right. You know the story you made up in your head that made you feel alone in the world.

Spiritual Classrooms

Relationships are spiritual classrooms, and we attract teachers to teach us what we need to learn about ourselves. These teachers are commonly disguised as a former spouse or mate, baby's daddy, disobedient child, irresponsible parent, disrespectful sibling, evil boss or co-worker, or annoying, soon-to-be-ex-best friend. One of the key indicators that you are functioning in a spiritual classroom is determined by your level of discomfort in a significant relationship.

The onset of discomfort is the primary indication that you are being positioned to grow in some area of your life. Whether it is spiritually, emotionally, physically, financially, or socially you can rest assured an opportunity to experience personal growth will soon be knocking at your door, and it's unlikely you will find it pleasant in the beginning. In fact, your immediate reaction may be to run for cover, or isolate yourself by leaving your job, relocating to another city, or taking on a massive project. Maybe you attempt to avoid the situation by busying yourself working overtime or volunteering, ignoring phone calls, text messages, and emails. Maybe you try to hide your insecurity or discomfort by overcompensating and taking on additional responsibilities that you know are going to send you over the edge, or spending more than you earn to keep up with the Jones's, or having someone on the side as a backup plan in case your significant other "acts up."

~ 91 ~

If you want to know if you're hiding, do a self-examination of your internal landscape to determine where in your life you're doing too much or being excessive and that will give you some clues to your behavior. Then apply the *Five Whys Problem-Solving Technique* to determine the root cause of your motivation. This technique can be used to understand the root cause of any of your maladaptive coping behaviors that manifest when you're confronted with an uncomfortable situation. You simply identify the problem or maladaptive behavior and ask yourself why five times to get to the root of the problem or your motivation. Below are the responses to one of my Five Whys Problem-Solving sessions, which I did to determine why I was habitually late to work:

Problem/Maladaptive Behavior: I am chronically late to work. (Avoidance)

Why? I hate working as a finance coordinator.

Why? It's boring.

Why? I stare at spreadsheets all day doing account

reconciliations and analyzing numbers when I'd rather help individuals solve personal problems and set goals.

Why? I experience the most joy from teaching people how to heal and live a purpose-driven life.

Why? Because I feel called to be an encourager and I can be of greatest service to God as a life coach!

After several additional Five Whys sessions, I learned that my morning activities, which included meditation, journaling, reading, and bathing, consumed a large chunk of my time. I needed this routine to sustain a positive mindset in preparation for work. I found so much joy and delight in my morning activities that I wanted to recreate that experience for others. I felt like I was on an adrenaline high. Even throughout my workday, I continued to journal. Regular work tasks that should have taken two hours or less took me twice as long because I could not focus on the task at hand; I was still relishing in my morning revelations and compiling notes for future personal development workshops and seminars.

The Spiritual Lesson of Honesty

Consider your past relationships. Were your former companions similar in some ways? Did they have similar strengths and challenges or likes and dislikes? Did they annoy you in the same ways? Did they have the same complaints about you? If you answered yes to any of these questions, then you may have repeated some spiritual lessons in your relationships. Many people tend to learn the value of honesty after they have experienced dishonesty. Though one may think it is okay to tell a small lie, the rippling effects can be just as devastating as a big lie. After all, who determines the quality of a lie—the offender or the victim? A lie is still a lie, regardless of the purpose it serves.

When it comes to discussing the virtue of honesty it is important to be transparent about your truth and who you are. You must be willing to identify your personal triggers, strengths, challenges, likes, dislikes, thoughts, and feelings. You must acknowledge your role in relationships that contributed to unexpected outcomes. You have to take responsibility for creating relationships that either supported your healing or didn't. And you have to own the mistakes you made that created disharmony.

Honesty as a spiritual lesson is about being self-aware and recognizing how you are the creator of your life experiences. Honesty is about accepting yourself as you are, flaws and all. It promotes a level of self-knowledge that requires you to be accountable for your creations. Honesty requires you to do a self-assessment to determine your core beliefs about who you say you are, who you think you are, and who you really are. Honesty forces you to reflect on your experiences and evaluate your current position in significant relationships versus where you want to be. Honesty helps you identify barriers or self-imposed limitations that may be hindering your progress.

In previous chapters I shared how my relationship with one man taught me a spiritual lesson, however, the lesson of honesty required three teachers. God thought it was important for me to learn the lesson of honesty so much that He used three gentlemen to teach this lesson. Each teacher, unique in his own right, was an involuntary participant. Our relationships were brief, and God used them to demonstrate the ways in which I sabotage myself. In my encounters with these men, I was dishonest and misleading with hidden agendas. Quite frankly, I was consumed with a victim consciousness, seeking revenge for the pain and suffering I experienced in previous relationships. My intentions with these men were out of character. I behaved in unloving ways that were contrary to my beliefs about love, relationships, and sex.

Shortly after my breakup with Unconditional Love, I started attending local community forums and social events to fill the void of being single yet again. I wanted to numb the feelings of disappointment and embarrassment of what appeared to be another failed relationship. Unconditional Love and I were very active in the community; we attended fundraisers and private events hosted by my company. We were recognized as a loving pair amongst our family and friends and I wholeheartedly believed that we would get married. Marriage was a part of our regular conversation and he agreed to adopt my children if they were still minors when we married. I even considered having a child for him since he did not have any. He was my soulmate and I was willing to do almost anything for the sake of our relationship.

Despite my best efforts, my relationship with Unconditional Love ended when we stopped communicating. It was our candid ability to discuss anything that made our relationship unique, so to end it without proper closure was unsettling. I called him one morning, after not hearing from him for a while, and he said he was having breakfast with a friend and that he would call me back. Immediately, my insecurity and ego thoughts surfaced: *We haven't talked in weeks and you're going to put me off until later, while you have breakfast with someone that you can see any time; I'm out of town and probably won't be able to see you until the next holiday. Oh, hell no! You don't ever have to worry about me, because I will not answer your call. You're probably with a woman. Nope, I won't wait for your return call and I definitely will NEVER call you again—I'm done!* Just as quickly as my thoughts raced, our passionate, two-year relationship dissolved without warning or opportunity for closure. Unconditional Love called several months later to wish me Merry Christmas, and that was the last time we talked.

I refocused my energy on local community outreach and engaged residents to participate in Love Campaigns. Although I was upset about my breakup, I could not negate the love I'd experienced in our relationship. It was unmatched and I was undeniably more loving, more compassionate, and more forgiving because of it. I couldn't help but to find other means to express my energy.

Throughout the Love Campaigns, I met some interesting people. One gentleman was seeking to create employment opportunities, mentoring, and recreational activities on the east side. We would often see each other at local events. In the beginning, our interest in each other was strictly platonic. We were exploring ways in which we could collaborate on different projects and share resources. He wanted a grant to get a facility and I wanted funding to run programs. We had somewhat similar funding goals that connected us. We started spending more time together, and eventually, we lost sight of our projects and fostered a personal friendship.

Nick was divorced with joint custody of his two sons. He served a couple of years in the military and was currently working as an engineer. He was boisterous, and his Mike Tyson physique was evidence that his bark was as loud as his bite. Although he had an aggressive personality, he was genuinely a sweetheart and big teddy bear. We courted for about two months before he wanted to date exclusively. I was flattered that he was interested, but it was too soon for me to commit. I hadn't gotten over Unconditional Love yet and I secretly longed for him to call and rekindle our relationship. Even though I knew Nick was seeking a committed relationship, I was not. I misled him to believe we were headed toward commitment when, I had no plans of ever being in a committed relationship with him. I was dishonest and not forthcoming with my thoughts and feelings about our friendship.

Occasionally, Nick would text provocative messages, to which I playfully responded. I had no intention of performing the explicit acts I described. I was just experimenting with a new form of communication that I thought was fun and harmless. I didn't know that Nick was serious. His descriptive details about licking, sticking, pulling, holding, and caressing were real talk, and he felt I had played with his emotions.

The truth of the matter was that I was afraid to entertain a relationship with Nick because of his strong personality. He used vulgar language, not because he was upset, but because it was a preference. His demeanor was threatening, not because he was intimidating, but because he was a big guy. He was assertive, explicitly asked for what he wanted, and was not afraid to voice his disappointment if he didn't get it. He was rigid with his passionate thoughts and opinions, which he vehemently defended as "not a sign of conceit, but confidence." While Nick was confident and sure of himself, I increasingly felt uneasy in his presence, which was ironic, considering he had the attributes I desired for myself. Nick was truly a great catch, and yet, I felt intimidated. Unfortunately, I wasn't wise enough to explore the feelings that surfaced in that relationship, or the Divine Invitation presented to grow and learn in the spiritual classroom. I chalked my feelings up to being symptomatic of my experience with domestic violence, and I reverted to my old tactics of withholding and denying my feelings.

Ultimately, I ended the courtship and told him I wasn't ready to move forward, when really, I was scared to confront my feelings.

How often are you dishonest about your thoughts and feelings? Do you answer truthfully when someone asks, "How are you doing?" Do you automatically reply, "Good," regardless of how you really feel? When a close friend intuitively asks, "What's up?" because they sense something is going on with you, do you answer truthfully or do you blow them off and say, "Nothing"? Can you recall a time when your child asked, "Mom, what's wrong? You look sad". Did you respond truthfully, or did you lie to shield them from your personal frustrations? When your supervisor asks if there is anything you would like to discuss, or if you need help completing a project, do you answer truthfully or do you pretend to have everything under control? When your spouse asks if there is anything on your mind that he should know about, do you answer truthfully, or do you wait until you're pissed off to address an issue that has been festering for weeks? When a client asks for your expert opinion, do you tell the truth, or do you hold back to protect her feelings because you think she can't handle the truth?

In each seemingly small communication, you can choose to be honest and upfront, or dishonest and misleading. Whenever you lie you invite distrust, pain, and guilt into your life. Dishonesty is a relationship thief. Dishonesty interrupts your ability to bond with others and build authentic connections. Dishonesty erodes your self-esteem and confidence and steals your joy. Although the truth can hurt at times, a lie will surely rob, cheat, and destroy you and your significant relationships.

Divine Invitations

God has an interesting way of teaching us what we need to learn about ourselves through relationships. Usually, the thing we dislike the most about others is the very thing we need to recognize and understand within ourselves. When I met Nick, I was not confident or assertive. I was a people pleaser. I sought external validation. I wanted to be liked by everyone and Nick was quite the opposite. He was more concerned with people understanding his personal worldviews and he challenged opposing opinions. He welcomed controversy, whereas I wanted everyone to be agreeable. In my spiritual classroom, God used Nick to model the character traits of self-assurance and confidence.

Since I didn't get the initial lesson God put in my path, I was afforded another opportunity. This time, the messenger was more appealing. I met him at a club in downtown Syracuse. He was performing as an exotic dancer. His name was Marcus and he was a native of West Africa and lived in New York City. He was intriguing. He spoke five languages and was working on an album. He wanted to hook up after the show, but I gave him my phone number instead. I figured if there was real interest outside of the club scene, he'd call me. Marcus called regularly and we hit it off. Our conversations were delightful, and it was a treat to hear his French accent. He was an up-and-coming artist, had several You Tube videos, co-founded a not-for-profit organization in West Africa and mentored his younger brother. His motivation was supporting his family back home. He wanted to expand the services of his youth organization.

Even though Marcus was focused and goal-oriented, he was not without flaws. Emotionally, he appeared reserved and shy. He was vocal about many things, except when it came to his personal feelings. He seldom discussed a desire for intimacy and mentioned little, if anything, about his past relationships. He was guarded, and that made our conversations feel impersonal. Marcus and I continued to talk over a period of months with no specific purpose in mind other than to chat.

After reevaluating my friendship with Marcus, I noticed similarities between this relationship and my courtship with Nick. The roles, however, were reversed. I was the aggressor and Marcus was passive and withholding feelings. I was vocal and upfront about my attraction and he seemed flattered. He always called me, so I assumed he was at least interested in getting to know me. Honestly, it didn't matter whether he was attracted to me or not because this was my pursuit—I considered it a game. I wanted to avenge myself for past failed relationships. I wanted to play the field for a change and get rid of the goody-two-shoes persona. I was a responsible, grown woman, and if I wanted sex, I should be able to have it.

After some time, Marcus and I connected in New York City. I attended a friend's birthday party and asked him to join me. I wanted to sleep with him. He was gorgeous, available, and had a body like Morris Chestnut. After being celibate for nearly two and a half years, I was ready for pleasure. Somewhere along the way, in a barrage of self-pity and anger, I decided to act like a man and pursue casual sex. I wanted to learn how to connect with men on the physical level and not engage emotionally. I hated that I felt the need to be in committed relationships before experiencing pleasure. I was tired of my traditional belief that sex is best between a married couple. I wanted to be free from the dreams I had of a fairytale love affair. I wanted revenge and I wanted the world to know I was stepping out of my comfort zone and pursuing men. I boasted with friends about my desire for Marcus. I wanted word to get back to my exes that I was out of the gate now. I wanted the men I'd loved to feel my wrath after freely giving my innocence to them and spending years investing time into our relationships. I was hurting and, as they say, *hurt people, hurt people*, or we try to.

Determined to make my short weekend getaway to NYC worthwhile, I tried to entice Marcus throughout the evening. I flirted with other men at every opportunity and pretended I was the guest of honor. On the dancefloor I tried to recreate the popular scene in the classic movie, *Dirty Dancing*. If only for one night, we were the celebrity couple. I introduced Marcus to one of my friends and she agreed that he was as fine as the tea in China. With her blessing, my plan to seduce him was solidified.

Marcus and I chatted and danced for hours before catching a taxi to his apartment at three in the morning. His place was small, and he lived with a roommate, which I didn't know about until we arrived at his apartment. Fortunately, his roommate was not home. We were exhausted and didn't waste any time heading for the bedroom. The chemistry we shared on the dancefloor made me feel more connected to him, and that made the final activity of the evening feel so right. He was a perfect gentleman. We rushed out later that morning because Marcus had to go to work. He gave me a quick tour of his mini home studio, and then we stopped for breakfast sandwiches and hopped on the train. He lived in Harlem and I was staying with a friend in Queens. When we arrived at his stop, we kissed and parted ways and that was the last time we saw each other. I felt accomplished.

Marcus and I remained phone buddies for several months after our rendezvous. He made plans to spend a weekend with me and then he canceled at the last minute. I spent a week preparing for his visit—cleaning, mopping, and dusting in areas I hadn't seen in years. Since he wooed me in the bedroom, I figured the least I could do was impress him with my domestic skills by having a meticulous home, just in case we wanted to take this friendship to the next level. Although I was pissed and disappointed, I wasn't too surprised when he canceled. In the back of my mind, I questioned whether he was genuine in his intention to visit, especially when he didn't mention his travel arrangements earlier that week. Had he visited, I would have paraded him around town in hopes that gossip and rumors spread to my exes. I was still in game mode and Marcus was my pawn. Shortly after he canceled, I ended our yearlong fling. If he didn't think enough of me to visit, then there was no need for me to continue the relationship—I'd already achieved my goal. I deleted his phone number from my contacts and ignored his calls. Eventually, he got the message. There was no love lost because I had achieved official player status.

As if Nick and Marcus weren't enough to teach me the error of my thinking, God sent Lewis to solidify the lesson in Honesty. He was someone to whom I'd been attracted for years. He was a community activist, author, and artist, and we'd flirted on and off for over five years. The timing was never right for us to explore our attraction because one of us was always dating someone. However, that didn't stop us from checking statuses whenever we ran into each other at events.

Lewis was educated and well-versed in many topics. His conversations were deep, and his intelligence was mesmerizing. He made love to my mind on many occasions. He captivated my attention with his words and beautiful smile. To describe him by his physical appearance would be a disservice, even though he would give LL Cool J a run for his money. It's no surprise Lewis had that effect on me—after all, he was close friends with Forgiveness in high school. They used to play football together, shared remarkably similar worldviews and lifestyles, and were both self-taught scholars in their own right.

Soon after my fling with Marcus ended, I turned my attention over to Lewis. This time around I didn't care if he was in a relationship, as long as he wasn't married. I planned to bait him and have a little fun. Lewis attended an event I hosted at my house. As planned, he was the last guest to leave, which gave us an opportunity to talk. We only saw each other at events, which made it difficult for us to engage in private conversations. Whenever we spoke, it was always about business or politics; we seldom had casual conversations. It was nice to finally explore our attraction. The next evening, he planned to come over and give me a massage. Offering a massage is probably the oldest trick in the book to get a person's clothes off. And I was all for it! He could give me a massage, bathe me, and put me to sleep if he wanted to. I simply wanted an evening with Lewis all to myself. No stage, no audience, no fanfare, just me and him alone, free to creatively explore our sensuality through foreplay. My girlfriends were excited for me because they knew he was a work in progress, and that we'd been flirting for years. They were my biggest cheerleaders.

It's ironic how much support you have when you are acting in self-destructive and unloving ways. I don't think my friends knew how angry I was with my exes. I'm sure they wanted me to be happy, and if casual sex was the new item on my to-do list, then they supported me. I wish I could have been honest with myself, my friends, and the men I was involved with. I didn't really want casual sex. I didn't really want to be a player. I didn't really want to hurt my exes. Besides, they were probably over our relationship and on to the next one. Usually, it is women who need closure and recovery time between relationships, not men. What I really wanted more than anything was attention. I wanted to be held and comforted until the wee hours of the morning. I wanted to be reassured that I was loved and important. I wanted a man to stimulate me mentally with conversation. I wanted every part of my body touched and caressed as if I was the most precious jewel on earth. I wanted to be relieved of the superwoman syndrome just for one night. In all honesty, sex was not my ultimate goal. It was a sacrifice I was willing to make to have intimacy with a man with whom I was not otherwise involved. I'd lost hope in finding Mr. Right, so I was willing to settle for Mr. In-the-Moment to get through the feelings of loneliness. I concealed my real feelings by believing I wanted revenge, when the truth was, I wanted to feel loved. Being a single mother, at times felt like the weight of the world was on my shoulders. I worked full-time, attended classes, volunteered, and was an entrepreneur. I had many roles and responsibilities that I valued and appreciated. I had a son and daughter who needed me to be nurturing, loving, strong, healthy, resourceful, creative, encouraging, present, and playful. But guess what? I desperately wanted the same loving support from a man, and I didn't have the courage to ask for it.

Lewis arrived just after ten that night. I cooked him a nice pasta dinner—he practiced a somewhat clean lifestyle. He didn't eat meat, drink alcohol, use drugs, smoke cigarettes, or frequent nightclubs. He practiced martial arts and associated with like-minded people. On the other hand, he apparently did not practice safe sex because he had multiple children by different women—I later learned he had one on the way.

Dinner was brief because the main course was to be served in the bedroom. I could not believe that Lewis and I were heading to my bedroom. It felt like a dream come true. I felt embarrassed, because once we entered my bedroom, I had no idea what I was going to do next.

Lewis and I engaged in foreplay for hours, followed by breathtakingly passionate sex like one of the scenes in *Zane's Sex Chronicles*. After our bubble bath, we laid in bed and talked about our dreams, goals, and business ventures. He attentively listened to every word and reassured me that success was inevitable if I followed my heart. He shared jewels of wisdom from his personal experiences as an artist and author and he volunteered to introduce me to community leaders with similar interests. Exhausted from talking, he kissed me ever so gently on my lips, my breasts, and the small of my back. Then finally he held me in his arms until sunrise and served me breakfast in bed.

That would have been one incredible night had that been my real experience, but it was not. In fact, my real experience wasn't even close. From the moment we entered my bedroom it was awkward. After years of anticipation, this was my moment, and I felt disconnected from Lewis. There was no chemistry between us. Whatever I had envisioned for this evening vanished upon entering the bedroom. Whatever I thought we were about to do no longer felt comfortable. I was going through the motions—I'd put myself in a position where I did not feel I could have a last-minute change of heart. I pursued him, and I'd thought I wanted him until we were actually on my bed, stark naked. I said, "This isn't right." We paused, made eye contact, and slowly separated. He got dressed, said a few words, hugged me, and escorted himself out.

I was royally ashamed by my behavior, attempting to treat men like pawns and play the field. I had too much self-respect and self-love to intentionally inflict pain on others. The only one hurt by my behavior was me. That is the beauty of relationships in the spiritual classrooms. They gift us with opportunities to reflect on personal choices and behaviors that result in undesirable outcomes.

I was dishonest with my thoughts, feelings, and desires, and God used Nick, Marcus, and Lewis to teach me the value of honesty, which allowed me to process my experiences of disappointment and uncover the many ways in which I was denying my feelings and dishonoring myself. What I learned after my dealings with my three gentlemen teachers was that I was not emotionally available or prepared to be involved with anyone. I needed to spend time alone to learn more about myself and invite God into the process. I made a conscious choice to surrender to and trust God. I intended to sit in the passenger seat and let God steer the way. I trusted that whatever He brought forth would be for my good.

1. Identify your fears and how you see yourself as a victim and communicate that to your partner.
2. Own your feelings and take 100% responsibility for what you feel.
3. Identify any unproductive habits that lead to self-betrayal and evaluate the pros/cons of changing your behaviors and remaining the same.
4. Speak your truth! Be truthful about your wants, needs and expectations.
5. Ask yourself often *"What am I feeling in this moment?"* and be willing to offer love and acceptance to yourself and communicate your feelings to others.
6. Choose to act with the highest level of integrity and self-respect.
7. Express compassion for yourself and others!

CHAPTER FIVE

Spiritual Lesson 5: You Will Experience Trust

*"It doesn't take a lot of strength to hang on; it takes a lot of
strength to let go."*
-J.C. Watts

People have the tendency to make the concept of trust about others, when it is really about your own ability to trust and believe in yourself, to know that no matter what life brings your way, you will survive because you are the beloved child of God. To reach this spiritual realization, you must go through a process.

Letting go can sometimes be the hardest thing to do in certain situations due to a variety of unknown factors. There is no way to predict the future with certainty, and for many, this may cause you to experience a sense of loss of control or fear and anxiety. Ever since I was about sixteen, I wanted to be in a long-term, committed relationship. I wanted an intimate connection with one man that would last a lifetime. My parents did it. They married young, and, despite trials and tribulations, they managed to remain committed. I was heartbroken when I realized that my first love, Forgiveness, and I would not be together forever. It became apparent the first time he struck me in the face while we were driving down the highway. I was holding our five-month-old son. It truly felt like my heart was ripped open.

Years later, I managed to move past the hurt and pain and make another attempt at having a committed relationship with Unconditional Love. This time, I'd been certain that God had sent me a soulmate to inspire me to love unconditionally. Convinced that we would marry and live happily ever after, I was disappointed again when that relationship ended.

Then there was Nick, Marcus, and Lewis, three men I pursued for all the wrong reasons, in the hopes of eliminating my desire for committed relationships. With this unsuccessful attempt, I was forced to be honest with myself about my desires and needs, and to honor my feelings, gain clarity for my personal choices, be still, have patience with myself, listen to the quiet voice within, and seek God for guidance on how to break the cycle of self-destruction. This process taught me to surrender—to let go of my yearning to be in a committed relationship and to trust God.

My decision to surrender and trust God was not about waiting on Him to provide a mate. It was letting go of my fixation on being in a relationship and what that represented. My desire for a mate stemmed from an insecurity that I was incomplete without a man. Being single meant something was wrong with me because I couldn't keep a man. In my eyes, being single once again meant public humiliation.

Even my brother noticed—he told me, "I don't know what's wrong with my sisters that y'all can't keep a man."

Unsure of whether he was joking, I replied, "I can't speak for them, but I'm waiting on God to prepare my man and I won't settle for less!"

But internally, I believed something *was* inherently wrong with me and I didn't want others to notice. I thought the best way to hide was in a relationship. Grateful for this awareness, I prayed to God and made myself a willing servant. I told God I would do His will and if that meant He needed me to be single, then so be it. I became a willing vessel, relieved of my fixation on marriage. To envision my future as a single woman, I had to accept defeat in the relationship arena. And nothing was further from the truth. I realized God had made me whole. I was not deficient and I did not need to be fixed. I was reminded of three simple truths I'd learned as a student at Inner Visions Institute for Spiritual Development (Inner Visions): I am the beloved child of God; I am the one in whom God is well pleased; I was created in the image and likeness of God.

Within days of my decision to surrender, I had a remarkable breakthrough and Divine Invitation. Astonishingly, I noticed my inner beauty project through recent photos I took for an assignment. The beauty shone through my headwrap, makeup, all white attire, and accessories. It was majestic, like an out-of-body experience. My soul was smiling and delighted that I'd finally noticed its brilliance—a quality I easily identified in others. It felt like a homecoming. At first glance, I was startled by my image in the picture. I didn't like taking pictures and for years I believed I wasn't photogenic. Instead of being in front of the camera, I hid behind other people. I didn't avoid the camera because I thought I was ugly—I avoided it because it was difficult for me to see myself beyond my flaws and imperfections. When I looked at myself in the mirror or in a picture, my attention was immediately drawn to flaws: a hair out of place, lint, a crooked smile, shiny forehead, bulging shirt, slanted jewelry—the list could go on and on. If I could see my flaws, then surely, everyone else could too, so I found it safer to stay away from the camera.

On this Divinely ordained day in May, I noticed my beauty and appreciated it. I was flawless. My soul had awakened. The same beauty that I praised in others was present inside of me. Imperfections and mistakes no longer defined me. I was free to make as many mistakes as were necessary to learn my spiritual lessons. I was about to embark on a new level of trust and faith. My outlook was bright and all-encompassing, and my self-esteem amplified. I began seeing myself as a conqueror. I was accomplished. I was successful. I was encouraged.

After my internal landscape shifted, I noticed beauty everywhere. People were friendlier, exchanging kind acts and gestures. There were more love stories on TV and at the movies. Self-improvement books provided step-by-step instructions on how to achieve and maintain peace, love, happiness, and success.

To Trust or Not Trust

Trust the process is what the faculty at Inner Visions often said to encourage us to move through the fear of vulnerability, step out of our comfort zone, and reclaim our inherited royalty as the beloved children of God. The faculty were our biggest supporters. Seeing how they loved us through the entire two-year personal development training, it was easy for me to learn to trust.

Previously, most of my spiritual lessons were delivered through my encounters with men. However, I developed the practice of trust as a student at Inner Visions, which was equivalent to earning a master's degree in learning and understanding oneself. Students were taught how to heal spiritual wounds and remember who they really were. Monthly classes were held in Silver Spring, Maryland with experiential learning, regular assignments, coaching and large groups. I learned how to take responsibility for my own healing and simultaneously developed a personal relationship with God.

When I enrolled in Inner Visions, I wanted to be a model student. The program required a financial investment and personal commitment. I already knew from participating in their other workshops to expect numerous Divine Invitations. So, I was excited about my acceptance into the program and eager to be recognized as an outstanding student.

During the Inner Visions first-year summer intensive at the Omega Institute for Holistic Studies in Rhinebeck, New York, I met Greg. He stood out because he was one of only four men in the program. Greg was appealing. He was suave, confident, and cocky. He had been through orientation before, so he was comfortable and relaxed, while the rest of us were attentive.

On the first night of orientation, God thought it was befitting to use Greg to initiate my spiritual classroom. At the end of class, everyone was instructed to complete worksheets, journal, and be in silence—we were not supposed to talk until breakfast the next morning. The instructions were not challenging for me, because I value journaling and quiet time. As an introvert, being with my thoughts is my favorite pastime.

I bumped into Greg in the lounge area in our suite. I was preparing to retire for the evening when he asked my name. Now surely, he heard the same instructions I did about silence. I decided, because of his good looks and sudden interest in me, to break my silence. It was like God sent him to entice me like the serpent in the Garden of Eden. So willing to fall from grace, I continued to make unloving choices in the hopes that Greg would notice and favor me amongst the other women in the program. In the blink of an eye, my goal of being a model student switched to being desired by Greg. It seems instinctive how quickly a woman will sacrifice personal goals for the attention of a man. Women are natural nurturers and most of us are taught to put other people's needs before our own. We take the backseat to support our mate, children, parents, colleagues, and friends, and we become the least important person on our lists. Greg was no exception—I made his need for instant communication more important than complying with instructions and completing my assignments. I catered to him, because he was, after all, an attractive man who could potentially 'choose' me and I didn't want to decrease my chances of being selected as his lady.

During the five-day intensive, Greg and I continued to get acquainted. He seemed like a breath of fresh air. He had a successful career, no children, and the fact that he was participating in the program made him appealing. By the end of orientation, Greg and I had exchanged contact information and became friends on Facebook. I was hopeful that our budding friendship would blossom into something more.

The program resumed three months later in Silver Spring. I was ready for a power-filled weekend. I put an extra oomph into my appearance since it would be a reunion for me and Greg. We hadn't spoken much over the summer, so I was looking forward to seeing him again. We saw each other briefly on the first night but didn't have a chance to speak. The next day, I expected to kick back and chill with him during lunch, but to my surprise, he didn't even acknowledge me. We went the entire weekend without having a conversation. *What happened?* I wondered. *Was he in a relationship? Did he begin dating someone else at Inner Visions? Was his interest during summer orientation superficial? Did I do or say something over the weekend to turn him off?* For the life of me, I could not figure out what I did wrong to be ignored.

On my five-and-a-half-hour drive home to Syracuse, I reflected—I'd dishonored myself when I'd decided to break the silence. I was disappointed with myself, not Greg. Greg was the instrument God used to facilitate the spiritual lesson. I started to berate myself for the poor choices I continued to make when dealing with men. It was apparent that when a potential male suitor was involved my common sense flew out the window, and I'd get caught up trying to win his attention. I just didn't feel important without it.

I was deeply enmeshed in a negative rant until I heard a small whisper say, *You witnessed a valuable lesson today. Does it feel good when you don't honor your commitments? Be gentle with yourself—you're learning. What's at the heart of the matter? Are you upset because you were ignored or are you upset because you lost focus? My precious daughter, you will have more loving opportunities to do a makeover; this is just the beginning.*

God has a habit of speaking to me so that I know it's Him. God softened my heart. After His gentle counsel, I focused on strategies to increase my success in the program. I considered current challenges for childcare, budgeting, studying, and spending quality time with my family, and devised solutions for the remainder of my drive. When I reached home, I had a strategic plan to meet the demands of this program and my primary responsibilities. In that situation, God used a displeasing situation for my good. It was never about Greg; it was a Divine Invitation to motivate me to create a plan for success. The goal was to focus on my healing and spiritual growth.

Inner Visions became my lifeline. The program was precisely designed so that every activity, detail, and service promoted healing. From the moment I pulled into the parking lot on the third Friday of every month until I departed on Sunday afternoon, my spirit was being rehabilitated through prayer, meditation, intention-setting, reflection, care-frontation, living vision plans, and relationship projects. I discovered faulty core beliefs. I revived dormant feelings. My mask was removed with each assignment, reading, and large group discussion. My faith increased with every mistake. My heart opened and I finally began to breathe. In vulnerable times, when I felt I could not relive one more memory of rejection and abandonment, or recall another experience of disappointment and heartache, just when I thought I would collapse from hearing another woman tell her story of pain and abuse, I was reminded to breathe. Breathing was my saving grace. The healing inner work at Inner Visions was challenging. It was like having major surgery without anesthesia. I had to go under the knife on many occasions to release toxic emotions, negative self-talk, and unproductive habits.

How often do you hold your breath when you're anxious or afraid? Breathing is probably the number one action people take for granted. It comes naturally, yet, when you are emotional, you forget to breathe. You hold your breath and exacerbate the situation. If you focus on your breath when you are distressed, you will calm down much sooner. The next time you're confronted with a difficult situation, pause and take three deep breaths before you respond. Allow your breath to be a reminder that God is in control.

In the process of healing at Inner Visions, I developed a personal relationship with God. He was an intricate part of my healing process. To trust the process meant that I surrendered control to God through small acts of faith. When you make a decision to do the inner work to become a better you, there will be many opportunities to practice your newly acquired skills. You'll be amazed at how quickly God tests your skills and I was no exception to this rule.

Less than eight hours after returning home from summer orientation, I received a call from my mother. She said she just called the ambulance for my father because he was having sharp pains in his chest and left arm. The pain woke him from sleep. She wanted me to meet them at the hospital. I called each of my siblings before rushing to the emergency room. My eldest sister lived out of town, and my other sister was keeping my children overnight. That left my brother and me at the hospital with my parents. An hour and a half passed before the doctor confirmed our suspicion that my dad had a mild heart attack. The doctor said we were "lucky" to have gotten him to the hospital when we did because it could have been worse. I told him, "It wasn't luck that saved him; it was God's mercy and grace, that spared his life."

The doctor told us that my father would be admitted because he needed a stent put in. The procedure would be performed in the morning. While we waited for a bed, all hell broke loose in the emergency room. My brother decided he wanted to interrogate my mother for choosing to call me, the youngest, and not him. He felt that, as the oldest and only son, he should have been contacted first. He furiously expressed that if something had happened to my dad, he would have blamed her and never forgiven her for it. My mom defended herself. My brother became enraged and started insulting her. He was yelling and acting inappropriately. My dad tried to intervene asking my brother to lower his voice, but he couldn't hear him. The alarm on the heart monitor sounded and my father sighed in pain. I watched each moment unfold before my eyes. I felt like a special guest with VIP access to a horror movie—it was insane. I had just played my first real-life role of "neutral observer" in what Inner Visions termed *the trio*. The trio consists of a *coach-* the facilitator in a situation, a *client-* the person seeking support, and *neutral observer-* the person holding the space and observing the conversation.

In all the turmoil and upset, I managed to remain calm and neutral. Not once did I comment or offer an opinion. I silently observed my brother verbally attack my mother out of hurt and fear. I watched my mother sit stoically and subject herself to verbal abuse. I was in shock and there was nothing I could say or do. Eventually, my dad asked my brother to leave and there was an awkward silence for what seemed like hours.

Outwardly, things seemed to calm down in the emergency room, but God was definitely brewing something for my spiritual growth. I didn't expect to practice my skills so quickly after orientation. And to my surprise, I passed the test. I could be in the midst of sheer hell and turmoil and not feel compelled to fix something because someone else is hurting. This is the art of trusting the process and surrendering control. I learned how to attentively listen; despite the traumatic ordeal my parents had experienced. I had to be mindful to not make that situation about them. It was a Divine Invitation for my spiritual evolution. My role was simply to hold the space by breathing and listening. Imagine if I had interjected in the argument—it would have appeared that I was taking sides, which would have created more chaos. Instead, I trusted God to work out the situation. Whatever wounds my brother had from childhood was between him and his parents. As the neutral observer, I was reminded that God has relationships with everyone, whether people choose to accept it or not. He heals, protects, directs and provides healing opportunities for others just like He does for me.

I've learned that being present during another person's explosive behavior does not automatically warrant my intervention. Sometimes I have to trust the process and let the situation unfold, unless there is imminent danger, in which case I would assist as much as possible. But trust demands a certain level of reliance on God. Everyone receives Divine Invitations and must go through their own spiritual evolution in order to heal. I just happened to be on a fast track course with God in the driver's seat.

Trusting God More

Seldom are you required to practice more trust than when you're dealing with matters pertaining to your children. You rear children in the ways you think are best, and when they deviate from your ideal pathway, you worry about their wellbeing. You forget that, once upon a time, you were rebellious, searching for identity, and trying to navigate life with limited knowledge and a know-it-all attitude. Perhaps you thought your parents were against you and wanted to ruin your life, or maybe you resisted parental advice because you believed they did not have your best interests at heart. Maybe you thought they didn't know anything because they had old-fashioned beliefs and traditions. DJ Jazzy Jeff & The Fresh Prince sums it up well in their song, "Parents Just Don't Understand." That's what many of us believed about our parents. They didn't understand our thoughts, our feelings or the peer pressure we experienced. They could not identify with our value system. And they definitely didn't remember that making mistakes were a part of life.

The ways of the world are drastically different from your early childhood. Now there is instant access to information via the internet, social media, reality TV, and more general access to people, places, and things that were once exclusive to the rich and famous. You may put enormous strain on yourself to lead your children on the path you think is best. You may obsess over protecting your children to the extent that you don't allow them to make mistakes. If they make a mistake, you assume you've failed them and experience a vicious cycle of guilt, shame and remorse. You recall toxic memories from your childhood. You vividly relive your experiences of abandonment, rejection, and invalidation. You ruminate over incidents that made you feel unloved. You recall the times your parents failed you and become convinced that you are just like them.

For some, the fear of becoming like your parents has come to fruition and you experience self-hate. This emotionally absorbing cycle is a Divine Invitation for you to trust in and surrender control to God. If you've done everything within your power to influence the circumstances of your child's situation, then trusting God is the next step. Trust God to take control. Trust God to provide your child with direction and guidance. Trust that God is working on behalf of your child just like He is working on your behalf. Trust and believe that the omnipotent, omniscient, and omnipresent God knows exactly what your child needs to develop his or her gifts and talents to carry out their purpose in the world. Trust that God, the Most High, who created the world, can surely establish a personal relationship with your beloved child as He did with you.

As quickly as you recalled the toxic memories of disappointment, remember the infinite ways in which God has protected and guided you through your formative years. Do you recall when God spared your life after an accident or illness in childhood? Can you recall when God answered your prayers for reconciliation with friends or loved ones? Do you remember how He helped you recover after flunking out of college or getting fired from a job? What about the time He helped you repair your credit? Did He ever save you from an eviction? How did God provide for and protect you as a teenager or young adult, when your parents did not know what else to do? You can rest assured in knowing that God has a plan for all your loved ones, including your beloved children. He will never leave or forsake you, despite what it may look like. Trust is developed through the practice of surrendering control.

The Spiritual Lesson of Trust

During the course of my study at Inner Visions I worked to develop a personal relationship with God, and through my relationship with God, I developed trust—trust in God, trust in myself, and trust for others. I became aware of how I was trusting or not trusting, and the moments in which I was not trusting were Divine Invitations for me to develop the spiritual fortitude to grow beyond my comfort zone. Through each observance of God's mighty power, my faith increased and so did my personal relationship with Him. He was my source of peace and calmness, hope and inspiration, and He never disappointed me. God was the one constant in life. I seized every moment as an opportunity to practice trust—at work, at home, and in all relationships—growing my confidence along the way. I made decisions and commitments with good intentions and believed that whatever the outcome, God was working on my behalf for my greatest good. I abandoned the notion of bad experiences and misfortune in search of lessons and blessings that presented Divine Invitations to practice trust.

There were several strategies that helped me build my trust muscle. I invite you to practice them. Implement one strategy daily, weekly, monthly, or all at once. Each approach is powerful in its own right and will transform your thinking and help you develop trust as a daily part of your spiritual regimen. I strongly recommend you document your spiritual growth with a journal. You'll be amazed by your evolution and spiritual transformation. You will begin to notice how the Holy Spirit is guiding you and opening doors for you. You will tap into wisdom you didn't know existed. You will unlock hidden gifts and talents. You will begin to connect with your higher self and others in more purposeful ways. And the journal will be evidence of your personal growth. If you only remember one thing from this chapter, let it be to keep calm and trust God when all else fails.

Seven Strategies for Developing Trust

1. Follow your inner guidance. Act on your intuition or "gut" feeling.
2. Pray and seek God* for clarity. Practice meditation or a spiritual regimen.
3. Express your authentic feelings.
4. Keep a journal.
5. Have a desire to trust and believe that you can do it.
6. Trust the process and surrender control. Be patient with yourself while you are developing this new skill.
7. Believe that God* is working on your behalf.
   Based on your own understanding.

PART III

THE DELIVERY

CHAPTER SIX

"Faith is taking the first step even when you don't see the whole staircase."
-Dr. Martin Luther King, Jr.

Faith can mean many things to many people. It can be a religious belief, a form of self-confidence or belief in a supernatural power or unseen force. Faith can define your religious traditions, or it can be a guiding principle for everyday living. Experience has taught me that faith is putting your ultimate trust in God to provide, protect, and perform for your greatest good. To have faith means that you recognize God's ability to intervene on your behalf. When you have faith, you believe beyond a shadow of doubt that all is well regardless of precedents, science, doctor's reports, credit scores, occupation, education level, socioeconomic status, sexual orientation, or disability. You wholeheartedly believe that with God, all things are possible. When you practice faith, you apply the spiritual principle of trust in your daily decision-making, especially when your circumstances appear bleak.

As an evolved soul, I have adopted faith as my guiding light. My decisions are based on the premise that God is always with me, and with Him I can conquer all. Faith is not an activity or something I practice occasionally—it's my mindset. Faith is my foundation. I trust God one thousand percent and I trust my spiritual evolution. Everything that pertains to me has a spiritual lesson attached to it. With every undesirable outcome, disappointment, inconvenience, setback, and delay there is a hidden lesson, blessing, or opportunity—a Divine Invitation.

My faith allows me to step out of my comfort zone and pursue great achievements that would otherwise paralyze me with fear. With faith, I can climb hurdles, stay the course, and move mountains. I have become spiritually wealthy and abundantly blessed. Without faith, I am reduced to smallness, limited thinking, and unfulfilled dreams. Without faith, I cannot have peace of mind during turmoil. Without faith, I could not unleash my creativity and fulfill my purpose. Without faith, every challenge would move me further away from God. Thankfully, God created me with a heart full of faith. Whenever I see or hear the word faith, my heart skips a beat. I'm like Pac-Man with his power pellets when it comes to faith—any mention or sight of the word faith excites and energizes me.

One of my responsibilities in this lifetime is to share with the world the miraculous power of having a faithful relationship with God. Some people put their faith in man and experience disappointment when people do not meet their expectations, which is a normal human response. However, when you put your faith in God, you will have a different experience, because God can do what people cannot. God is consistent, forgiving, merciful, patient, loving, understanding, and always in Divine time. His spiritual lessons will transform your pain into passion, and your passion into purpose. God will convert your mess into a message of hope and inspiration. God will help you overcome disappointment, grief, and loss. You simply need to have faith in God's ability to use you just as you are and trust the process.

Although it feels like a lifetime ago, I didn't always have unyielding faith. It was cultivated while attending Inner Visions. I healed negative core beliefs and recognized my status with God. I developed positive self-trust and learned to pray and intercede for my own well-being. I was an active student of the universe armed with spiritual principles, tools, and affirmations that reminded me of my truth. I began to believe in my ability to recover from setbacks. I recognized that, with flaws and all, I am still beautiful in the eyes of God. My mantra was, *I am the one in whom God is well pleased.* I consulted God more often through prayer and meditation. During prayer, I cried out to God and released my concerns, frustrations, desires, and challenges; during meditation, I listened for His answers. For complex situations, I would fast to experience a deeper connection with God. I learned to discern God's voice among the silent chatter in my head. We developed a beautiful relationship. God was my main squeeze; our partnership was profound. I was an obedient student and I trusted Him. Whatever He asked of me, I obliged, even if I didn't believe in my ability to carry out the task. In those uncomfortable moments, I used journaling to cope with my feelings, questions, and concerns. It was very useful. I had a record of God's unusual requests and months later, I was able to put the pieces together. It was proof of the existence of something much greater than I could possibly imagine intervening on my behalf. Faith is my life source, my hope, and my inspiration. Faith is the thing that shapes my very existence and my personal relationship with God.

Walk-on-Water Faith

When you make a commitment to God to be a faithful steward, you will be tested. This is true for anyone who desires a personal relationship with God as they lead a purpose-driven life.

While my faith was mature when God instructed me to resign from my job, where I had worked for nearly nine years, and enroll in graduate school, I was still anxious about His direction. I hesitated to submit my resignation. At first, I asked my manager if part-time was an option for my position and undoubtedly it was not. Before asking, I knew part-time was not practical. That was my attempt to insert my will over the situation. In fact, God was clear in His instructions. He said, *My daughter, I know you are faithful, but I want you to develop walk-on-water faith.* God has an interesting way of calling me out of my comfort zone. It's not like I haven't asked for it. My constant prayer and affirmation is that *I am of service to God.* I want to be used for His purpose to spread love by all means available. Therefore, it is never a surprise when God honors my request to do His will.

For years, I'd wanted to work in the area of my passion—personal development and human services—develop my life coaching practice, and turn my volunteer services into a profitable business. Releasing my job was the first required act of faith. In obedience to God, I submitted my resignation and entered the world of unknowns. I was unsure how soon I could create an income from my coaching services. I didn't know how long my savings account would sustain me. And I definitely didn't know what God had planned for my future. So, I followed God's instructions and practiced *walk-on-*

water faith, trusting God to provide at every step on my new path.

Walk-on-water faith is the type of faith where you expect God to do the impossible. You expect a miracle. You expect a supernatural gift from the Source of all that is. When the blessing shows up, you and everyone around you will know it could have only been God. One key indicator that you are exercising walk-on-water faith is the intensity of your expectation that God is doing the impossible in your life. This kind of faith requires total reliance on God as you approach uncharted territory. You will feel outside of your comfort zone, and at first glance, nothing will seem familiar. You may even feel inadequate or think you are ill-equipped to address a situation or perform a task because you lack the knowledge, skills, tools, or resources. However, when you are exercising walk-on-water faith, instead of focusing on your deficiency and acquiring the necessary skills, you proceed with confidence, knowing that no matter the outcome, you will not fail because God has your back. These acts of faith would be similar to jumping ship knowing you cannot swim, but trusting, believing and knowing that as soon as you hit the water, God will provide a way for you to survive. Hence, walk-on-water faith.

Faith is a spiritual muscle. It requires constant development and strength training through practice and application. As with any muscle, if you don't use it, over time, it becomes weaker. However, if used frequently, the muscle becomes toned and your strength increases. The same applies to your faith. Trials and tribulations are spiritual supplements that enhance your faith. After you overcome a trial, you feel good, accomplished, and encouraged. Your self-confidence grows and your belief in your ability to manage future trials grows. In many instances, you may face daily trials and tribulations that can be likened to daily vitamins. Similar to taking a multi-vitamin to boost your immune system, God will provide you with trials to exercise your faith muscle. On a daily basis, you have to decide how to respond to the adversities of life. Will you choose the path of victim or conqueror? Will you become defensive and attack, or will you put on your spiritual armor, exercise your faith muscle, and trust that God is working everything out in your favor?

Faith is an action; it is something you do. The saying, *faith without works is dead*, is true. You have to actively practice your faith. Just like exercising, you have to do it in order to experience the benefits. You cannot develop faith by simply waiting on God to fight your battles. You develop faith by acting as though you have already won. You face the fear, obstacle or challenge head on as if you have everything you need right now to achieve your desired outcome. If your goal is to purchase a house and you have less-than-perfect credit, as an act of faith, you would open up a new savings account, name it *New House Fund* and make regular deposits into the account. If you deposit ten dollars every week for one year, you will have saved five-hundred and twenty dollars toward your new house. After seeing your success, the second year you may decide to increase your weekly savings to thirty dollars a week and save one-thousand, five-hundred and sixty dollars in the second year. Now you've saved two-thousand eighty dollars and developed the discipline of saving. If you are a first-time homebuyer there may be additional money available to you through matched-savings or grants at your local banks and credit unions. After a few years of saving and small acts of faith to support your goal of home ownership, you will finally be paying a mortgage.

Walk-on-water faith requires you to take your faith to the next level, a level where you experience extreme discomfort, like being submerged in a tidal wave in the Atlantic Ocean. This level of faith is not about believing God will handle small challenges. Walk-on-water faith is trusting and knowing that God will do the impossible. It is knowing that God will grant you supernatural strength to remove a 3,500-pound vehicle from a child pinned underneath. It is knowing God will heal you from the generational curse of alcoholism without you attending A.A. meetings. It is knowing God will allow you to become a world-class leader with less than an eighth-grade education. It is knowing God will use your disability to teach people holistic strategies for coping with mental or physical illness. It is believing in your Divine calling to the point that, if you were forced to choose between your family and your calling, you'd choose your calling with the knowledge that God will provide you with a surrogate family. Walk-on-water faith is knowing that God will take you from homeless to Harvard. It is knowing that you can take one-thousand dollars and build generational wealth. Walk-on-water faith is knowing that even if you committed murder, you could develop a ministry working alongside the survivors of your crime. God can use anyone in any capacity to bring healing and compassion to His people. When exercising walk-on-water faith, you allow the Holy Spirit's presence within you to develop your optimistic appetite for identifying spiritual lessons, blessings, and opportunities.

Developing Walk-on-Water Faith

To develop a walk-on-water faith mindset, you must allow God to sow, harvest, and water seeds of optimism in your womb. Allow Him to use some of the most traumatic experiences in your life for His glory. You only have to be willing, and God can take it from there. *Are* you willing? Consider an event in your life where you felt violated or experienced injustice. What were your thoughts and feelings about the event? The people involved? How did you feel about yourself? What was the final outcome? Write down your responses below:

_____

_____

_____

_____

_____

_____

_____

_____

_____

_____

_____

_____

_____

For the next step you may have to dig deep, search your soul, and pray and meditate. But give it your best effort and be patient with yourself. You may need to repeat this step several times before you receive a response. Reconsider the same incident with the appetite for optimism that God is developing in you. Can you identify a spiritual lesson that you have learned, or a guiding principle you adopted as a result of the event? Deep down, underneath all the pain and suffering, was there a blessing in disguise? As a result of the event, did you change how you make decisions or adjust your lifestyle? Did you start any new initiatives, campaigns, or change careers? Do you see people or view the world differently? Write down your responses below:

_____

_____

_____

_____

_____

_____

_____

_____

_____

_____

_____

_____

Walk-on-water faith is not for the faint of heart. It is practiced by individuals who aspire to surrender their will in service to God. There is nothing easy or comfortable about exercising this type of faith. Your family and friends may perceive you as having "lost it" or "gone crazy." It is common for these individuals to declare that they and God are collaborating on projects. Individuals who practice walk-on-water faith understand that they are never alone. They acknowledge God as working within and through them. People who practice walk-on-water faith are seldom, if ever, worried about the future because they possess and profess an inner knowing that no matter what the future holds, all is well because God is with them. People who practice this level of faith are often characterized as spontaneous or extreme risk-takers. Some may even consider them irresponsible. But no matter how these individuals are perceived by others, they are clear that God is in total control. They are relieved from the stress and anxiety of having the weight of the world on their shoulders. They have extreme trust and faith in their ability to recover from any setback because they are purposefully working as a vessel for God.

The Experience

In the beginning, each day was different and pleasant. Upon waking, I waited for instructions from the Holy Spirit. I trusted my instincts and followed my heart, and that became my daily spiritual regimen. I expressed gratitude, sat in silence, meditated, listened for guidance, and wrote in my journal. Beauty unfolded in everything, doors opened, and opportunities seemed plentiful. Life was good. I was no longer in bondage to a job I hated. I practiced walk-on-water faith daily, knowing that what God had in store for me was for my greatest good. I felt fulfilled. Soon after I resigned from my job, I joined a small business resource center and took a business plan writing course. I worked with two business counselors to develop the blueprint for my personal development company. God ordered my steps and I developed supportive relationships with the counselors rather quickly. We had a friendship and mentorship that extended beyond the business resource center. Our relationship was reciprocal in that we benefitted from each other. They had strong professional backgrounds in business, accounting, marketing, and networking, and I was spiritually attuned, which allowed us to have insightful conversations about our callings, visions, and purposes. It was apparent that their desire for my personal success was as great as my own.

As if leaving a consistent source of income for the unfamiliar was not enough of a demonstration of walk-on-water faith, I also enrolled in graduate school out of obedience to God. I was at a pivotal time in my life and felt conflicted about my next steps. I had to decide whether to finish the program at Inner Visions, become an ordained minister, or pursue a master's degree in social work. I was confused because I felt like a failure at Inner Visions. I submitted assignments late, owed late fees, did not honor my commitments, and I did not see light at the end of the tunnel. I thought I was in jeopardy of failing my second year. And I loved the program. I didn't understand why I could not commit to my study schedule, submit assignments on time, or complete my project. I couldn't determine the root cause of my self-sabotaging behaviors and I wanted to quit Inner Visions. I decided I would rather quit before I failed the program. I wrestled with the decision for days because I knew I wasn't a quitter. I had a record of finishing everything I started, but the threat of failing overpowered my need for a blemish-free record. That's when I realized, I needed a Divine intervention. I needed God to intercede on my behalf. I could not pray this matter away and I could not solicit my prayer warriors. I needed and requested direct assistance from God.

One day, while sitting at my desk, I contemplated the decisions before me and sought God in an unusual way. I wrote each choice I was confronted with on seven small pieces of paper and put them in a cup. I prayed, meditated, and set an intention to receive guidance. I surrendered my will to God and asked Him to provide instructions for my next step because the lack of clarity and inability to make a decision was taking a toll on my body—I started having recurring migraine headaches, and I felt tired and overwhelmed. I couldn't focus at work—my mind was constantly wandering. I needed help and only God could resolve my spiritual dilemma.

During my prayer, I committed to God that I would adhere to whatever He decided for me. I asked a direct question: "What is my next step?" The piece of paper I pulled out of the cup read, *Enroll in graduate school.* From that Divine selection, I automatically knew what the following steps were. I completed the program at Inner Visions, left my job, applied to grad school, and started a new business. With each taste of success, my relationship with God and my faith grew stronger. I was comfortable relying on God to solve my problems. When setbacks or disappointments happened, I knew God was up to something. I knew He was preparing a

Divine Invitation for me to learn, or demonstrating an opportunity to prove, once again, His power. After a while, I embraced my challenges because I knew God would perform a miracle right before my eyes. He was using certain situations to develop my spiritual gifts and abilities to do His will in an even greater capacity. Some challenges were so intense it felt like God was giving me the doctorate level course; at least, that was what I told myself to cope and remain optimistic.

Positive Self-Talk

Developing walk-on-water faith requires positive self-talk— those encouraging conversations you have with yourself. It can be affirmative, such as: *I am a winner. I am confident and competent. I am a survivor. I am an heir to God's throne. I am the recipient of God's unconditional love, mercy, and grace.* With affirmations, you are declaring the condition or experience you want to achieve. You are speaking life into a situation and you believe what you affirm is true or can be true. You must believe in your statement at least fifty-one percent for real efficacy. According to Mahatma Gandhi, "Your beliefs become your thoughts, your thoughts become your words, your words become your actions, your actions become your habits, your habits become your values, your values become your destiny."

Affirmations, when applied deliberately and constructively, can help you weather a storm. In moments of despair, it is important to encourage yourself, and be reminded about the power of God, and that you are in His will. Positive self-talk can also be brief statements such as: *I can be anything I want to be. I can create the life I want to live. I can release ten pounds. I can beat this disease. I can climb to the top of the mountain. I can finish this race. I will be debt-free. I will be America's next top model.* Positive self-talk is about reminding yourself of your true essence. At the core of your being—your soul—you are a perfect, precious, beautiful child of God, a recipient of God's unconditional love, grace, and mercy. There is absolutely nothing you can do to get out of God's grace, love, and mercy. So, when your circumstances change or you make poor choices, it is important to use positive self-talk to remember your truth and foster walk-on-water faith.

What are you telling yourself when you are going through adversity? What do you tell yourself after you attempt to break an undesirable habit for the seventeenth time? What do you say about yourself when you end your relationship with Mr. Wrong? What do you believe about yourself when your adult children go astray? When you feel unappreciated or unloved, what lies do you tell yourself, or what stories do you make up to rationalize your feelings? Based on past experiences, if what you have been telling yourself in response to these self-inquiries has not made you feel encouraged, accepted, confident, or competent, you were not practicing positive self-talk. More than likely, you were feeling discouraged, hopeless, and depressed. Be aware of the difference between positive self-talk and negative self-talk. Positive self-talk makes you feel like, with God, you can conquer the world. Negative self-talk makes you feel like you are alone in the world.

Documenting Your Journey

Another useful approach to developing walk-on-water faith is documenting your journey. It is important to record your experiences in a file that you can reference easily. You can write entries in a journal, type them on your computer, or record them on devices. Documenting provides evidence of your life's progression. It is not necessary to write every detail of your life in a journal; however, it is important to record pivotal moments, intense feelings, trials, and triumphs. You should document when you feel compelled to do something out of the ordinary because that is a good sign that God is at work, inspiring you to get out of your comfort zone, think outside the box, and be innovative. It is a good idea to keep a small notebook with you at all times.

The beauty of documentation is that you will experience the cycle—you get to see how God is moving in your life, which will increase your reliance on and trust in Him. With increased faith, you lean on God more, your relationship with God grows, your trust in God grows, and you practice more faith. Documenting your journey will also show you specific examples of when God answered your prayers.

The Spiritual Growth Process

Positive self-talk and writing are solid ways for expanding your faith, but the essential growth for walk-on-water faith is action. You must put in the work with appropriate steps to activate walk-on-water faith. Sometimes, the hardest step in any change process is committing to action steps. Action steps are the necessary tasks that need to be completed to reach the overall outcome. Let's break down the elements of walk-on-water faith to understand the logical order of this process.

First, before you can develop walk-on-water faith, you must first have faith. You must believe in a Source or existence greater than you—for me, it is God. Second, there must be a situation, condition, event, need, or desire demanding your attention that is the *water*. Third, you must commit to action, whether that means relocating, changing careers, applying for a loan, starting a new business, or firing your boss—you must decide to take a stance and then *walk*. Walk-on-water faith is not as simple as one, two, and three. You have to be intentional, prayerful, and willing to rely on and trust God.

My son, Ra'el, had the privilege of exercising walk-on-water faith in the spring of his junior year of high school. He visited a college in Washington, DC. Prior to the tour, this college was the only school he was considering. He researched other schools and determined it was the best pick for a major in archeology. During the tour, he learned that tuition was over $56,000 a year for out-of-state residents, and if he applied for early decision and was accepted, he would be in a binding contract with the university, not contingent on financial aid packages or student loans. Early decision meant once he was accepted, he would legally and financially be obligated to attend. We decided early decision was not a good idea. However, that did not deter his goal to attend the university. After the visit, he constantly affirmed his future. He spoke as if he was already enrolled. He would say things like, "You are going to miss me when I'm in DC," or, "Once I'm there I can visit the White House daily if I want to." He highlighted articles in *National Geographic* magazines written by professors at that university. If you didn't know him, you would have thought he was a current student because of his esteem for the school. It was in a large metropolitan area with lots of networking opportunities for his interests. He said that he would always have something to do or somewhere to go. He applied to other colleges at the request of his guidance counselor, but he was determined to attend the university in DC.

One evening in November after dinner, Ra'el said, "Mom, I have a master plan! I know how to go to school for free, I'm going to join the Marines."

I chuckled because I thought he was joking. Never in a million years could I imagine him joining the armed forces. He just wasn't that type. He respectfully challenged rules, so joining the military and submitting to countless restrictions seemed out of his league.

I asked if recruiters had visited his school and he said, "Yes."

He explained the educational benefits, opportunities, and salaries as the selling points for his interest. He was willing to do whatever it took to attend school in DC. In the back of my mind, I thought this couldn't be the same son who detested chores, cleaning up after himself, and being asked to tidy his room before company arrived. There was no way my child, who said he was going to write a memoir about how dishes destroy families, was proclaiming he was going to join the marines. I was in total disbelief, but admittedly, he had a solid plan. It had to be a Divine Invitation.

Despite my opinions, I believed in his plan and, more importantly, *he* believed in it. God was providing him with an introductory course for walk-on-water faith and, although he was unaware of God's plan at the time, I was fully aware. Ra'el had passion, commitment and spoke life into his situation. He affirmed his attendance at the university, submitted an application, and made plans to attend in the fall. The first step in his course of walk-on-water faith was his belief in his master plan—he exercised his *faith*. He believed, without a shadow of a doubt, that he had the perfect plan to finance his college education at his dream school.

Next, he completed the application for the Air Force (after further discussion we both agreed that the Air Force would be a better fit). His desire, which was akin to the *water*, was to receive the commander scholarship for full tuition, room, and board, as well as a monthly stipend. This scholarship was only offered to one incoming freshman each year. After acceptance in the Air Force program, he interviewed with the Lieutenant Colonel at a local university and was offered the commander scholarship. Ra'el asked whether transferring the scholarship to the school in DC was an option; it was not. There was only one commander scholarship awarded at the local university and the student had to attend that university to receive it. The Lieutenant contacted the Lieutenant Colonel at the school in DC, but, unfortunately, the commander scholarship there had already been awarded. This posed a dilemma for Ra'el—he had two days to either accept or forfeit the scholarship at the local university. He came to me for advice. I decided to approach our conversation as a life coach instead of his mother. I had to silence my maternal instincts, which wanted to shield him from disappointment, for the sake of exploring his future goals and aspirations. I listened to him discuss the pros and cons and encouraged him to make a decision based on what he wanted for his future, instead of making a decision out of fear. I advised him to focus on his heart's desires instead of our financial situation, to make a decision based on what he wanted and not what he thought he could have, and to not limit himself to what was currently available.

After thoughtful consideration, he decided to decline the commander scholarship at the local university. He said he wanted a different experience, and if he attended that university, which was practically in our backyard, it would feel just like high school. As his coach, I supported his decision—I am a firm believer in pursuing one's dreams. I believe everyone can have what they want if they so desire. As his mother, however, I was initially concerned about finances. Secretly, I wanted to say, "Accept it, accept it, accept it, please accept that scholarship, son," until I realized Ra'el was practicing faith. He was demonstrating the skills I put into practice daily. He had made his second major decision—the first being joining the Air Force—and I could not have been prouder.

It was important for me to distinguish my role when he requested advice. I knew it would have been difficult for me to be objective from a mother's perspective because I was aware of our current finances and was experiencing my own fears and limited thinking. I had to assume the role of a coach to avoid projecting my insecurities and doubts onto my son. With his decision to decline the commander scholarship, his *walk* with God began. He had to experience ultimate trust and total reliance on God. Once you commit to walk you do not necessarily think about it. You continue to take the necessary action steps until you reach your desired outcome. In Ra'el's case, he submitted a freshman enrollment deposit, registered for summer orientation, and continued to tell friends and family that he would be attending the university in DC in the fall. Nearly two weeks after he declined the commander scholarship, he received a call from the Lieutenant Colonel in DC. He wanted to know if Ra'el was still interested in attending the university. He said the commander scholarship had become available and they wanted to interview Ra'el. Look at God!

Upon accepting the invitation to interview, there was a catch-22—the Lieutenant had less than a week to award the scholarship and the interview was in Washington, DC. It was Wednesday and the interview was scheduled for Saturday. Under normal circumstances, this would not have been an issue. But we lived in Syracuse and we were in the midst of a winter storm. In good faith, Ra'el confirmed the interview for Saturday, anticipating that I would drive him to DC early Friday morning.

Little did we know the wintery weather would worsen, my route being hit the hardest, making traveling to DC by car unsafe. Forced to make alternate arrangements, I purchased round-trip airline tickets. Thinking all was well, I felt relieved that his travel plans were finalized. The next day, we learned all fights from Syracuse to DC and surrounding areas were canceled due to the winter weather advisory. I started to grow anxious because now we only had two days to make other arrangements. I searched for bus tickets and couldn't find one that would get him to DC early enough on Saturday. Eventually, I found a train ticket that would leave early Friday morning and arrive in DC late Friday evening. I booked the last ticket and once again felt relieved that the quest was over. As a last resort, I figured I would plan to drive to DC early Friday morning if I had to even though I was terrified to drive in wintery weather. If it came down to it, I had made my mind up to confront my fear and take my chances if it would increase my son's chances for an academic scholarship.

We arrived at the train station early Friday morning, only to learn the train was delayed by an hour. We waited. Then we were informed it would be delayed another forty minutes. After waiting nearly two and half hours in the lobby, the train arrived, and passengers began boarding. I stopped Ra'el on his way to board, gave him a whopping hug, and whispered "Go claim your award!" Ra'el called later in the day to report he'd made it safely to New York City, and then the train broke down; they were waiting for another one to pick them up. Remember that walk-on-water faith is not for the faint of heart. With this level of faith, you will be tested when you are almost at the finish line.

The Lieutenant Colonel emphasized how important it was for Ra'el to make the interview on Saturday so that he could make a decision on Monday to prevent the forfeiture of the scholarship. As a rule, I do not believe in the concept of the devil. I do not believe in any force or entity having power equal to or greater than that of God. Yet, during this trial I started questioning if the devil was, in fact, real. Ra'el was experiencing setback after setback.

After several hours of waiting for another train, the passengers were picked up and Ra'el was once again heading to claim his award. He met his grandparents at the train station in DC late Friday night and spent the night at their house in Maryland. The next morning, they had breakfast and drove to the school. At some point, they got lost on their way, but they were able to reroute and arrive with a few minutes to spare.

The interview lasted about an hour. Can you believe that? Only one hour, after three days, one plane, a bus, and two trains. Reportedly, it went well, and he would learn of his fate in three days—there was at least one other candidate. Early Tuesday morning, Ra'el received a call from the Lieutenant and he was offered the Freshman Airman Commander Scholarship award. The scholarship covered tuition, room and board, meals, and a monthly stipend that could be used for books and miscellaneous expenses. He was awarded a full ride to his dream school in DC!

Walk-on-water faith is a process, and, as in my son's case, you will have setbacks, you will experience doubt, you will be tested, and you will have trials. And if you don't, then you should know you are not practicing walk-on-water faith.

Seven Steps to Develop Your Faith

1. Establish an understanding of God, Source, Higher Power, The Creator, The Most High, The Universe, Oneness or whatever term you deem appropriate based on your own understanding.
2. Schedule consistent time to study and learn more about God*.
3. Develop a personal relationship with God through prayer, meditation, fasting, journaling and other spiritual practices.
4. Believe that YOU are the beloved child of God in whom S/He is well pleased.
5. Start trusting and relying on God to help you make decisions.
6. Consult with God on all your decisions.
7. Wholeheartedly believe that God is working ALL things out in your favor!
    Based on your own understanding.

CHAPTER SEVEN

*"Courage is the willingness to trust God and practice faith in
every area of your life."*
-ArDenay Garner

There comes a time in your life when you have to take the first step in spite of your fear of the unknown. You will be faced with a choice to either maintain the status quo and do what you have always done or do something new that will require your absolute trust and faith in God. In this instance, you will have to "do it afraid," as Minister Joyce Meyers says in her book, *The Confident Woman*. Whenever fear is present, rest assured, you are being presented a Divine Invitation to practice courage.

When exercising courage, you are forced to gather the strength you developed from the previous six spiritual lessons of relationships to facilitate the advanced lesson of courage.

Courage requires you to practice Forgiveness—accept the past and bless it to avoid reliving toxic feelings or a similar situation.

Courage requires you to exercise Passion—be fervent, persistent, and committed to follow through on the thing that requires your attention.

Courage requires you to practice Unconditional Love— remember God loves you unconditionally, and that it is essential to love yourself and others while moving through your fears.

Courage requires you to practice Honesty—be honest about your desires and needs. And acknowledge your feelings and process them all the way through to continue to grow.

Courage requires you to exercise Trust—rely on God to see you through to victory.

Courage demands that you practice Faith—believe that with God, all things are possible, that you are a conqueror and can overcome adversity. Use courage to demonstrate a purposeful act of faith.

Courage requires you to take the spiritual lessons learned from past relationships and transform them into guiding principles that govern your daily life. Once adopted, these guiding principles will inevitably become your new core values that will alter your thinking, perception, and beliefs about people, places, and things.

There was a time in my life when I wanted a husband, a life partner, more than anything, because I was convinced that life would be easier to digest with a mate. I wanted someone with similar interests, characteristics, and desires. I wanted someone I could depend on, someone to support and encourage me. I convinced myself my knight in shining armor only existed in the South because the men I encountered didn't fit the bill. They had the intellect, education, income, but something was still missing. They were not interested in long-term relationships. They did not appear willing to take on a family of three and be providers. When I think of providers, I envision men like my father.

He's from Georgia. He paid all the bills while my mother spent her money on home décor, clothes, vacations, and stashed some in savings. She may have purchased a car or two, but he certainly spent his income on maintaining the household. And if he ever came up short, she had his back. That was their financial arrangement. The men I dated had a 50/50 rule—they believed household expenses should be split equally between couples. While that was not a terrible idea, it was not my vision. I am more traditional—I expect the man to be the head of the household and pay all the bills.

It was not just their view of finances; most of the Northern men I dated didn't want to get their hands dirty. When it came to repairing things around the house, they would rather hire someone to make the repair instead of fixing it themselves. I called it the "Northern man" syndrome—book smart but mechanically challenged. Let me be clear, I love Northern men—all men, for that matter—but in my experiences, the Northern men I dated could not fix anything with their hands. They could sell you a home or insurance, write books, perform on stage, read astrological charts, and motivate you to believe in yourself, but could not and did not want to learn how to repair a washing machine, install brakes on a car, fix a leaking faucet, paint, or put up sheetrock. Ever since Unconditional Love told me his adoptive father built the home his family lived in, I longed for that. I wanted a man who had the ability to build his own house. Imagine that—your man builds the house you live in with his bare hands.

Whenever I felt overwhelmed, I would fantasize about having a husband to help ease the burden of everyday life. I dreamt of crying on his shoulder while he embraced me and whispered that everything would be okay. I envisioned pillow talk conversations about work, family, and our dreams. I desperately wanted reassurance from a strong, loving man of my own that I was not alone, and that we were in this thing called life together. For several years after my relationship with Unconditional Love ended, there was not a day that went by when I did not long to have a husband. I wanted the companionship and security of a committed partnership.

My desire to have a husband spilled over into my personal development training at Inner Visions. I told my faculty advisor I wanted to move to Durham, North Carolina to find my husband. Why Durham, you ask? Was it a magical place filled with single and available Black men? Close, but not exactly.

During one of my family reunions, which was hosted in Durham, I attended a First Friday event at a major hotel in the area and partied with over three-hundred young Black professionals. It was an evening networking event and the men were as sharp as a tack. Judging from outside appearances, the men seemed to have their act together. I had a great time and even saw the comedian, Kevin Hart.

After discussing my ideas for relocating to Durham with my faculty advisor, I was warned that I wasn't ready for a husband and that I needed to identify one-hundred and five qualities I wanted in a man if I wanted to attract a mate. This was due at the next class, which was in about a month. Although I valued my advisor's wisdom as the eldest member of the faculty, I was perplexed. I couldn't help but wonder whether she was mistaken, or whether she really knew me. Quickly, I started assessing my situation: I had a house, a car, a job, was investing in my personal development, my kids were straight "A" students, and I lived drama-free. What more did I possibly need to be ready? Was there something inherently wrong with me? Was I too weak? Was I a pushover? Were my demands too much? Was I too headstrong? I wanted to know what this wise woman saw in me that convinced her I was not prepared.

My advisor reassured me that nothing was wrong with me. She said I was perfect just as God created me. She reminded me of how important it was to declare to the universe my ideal mate and questioned if I was prepared to receive him.

She asked, "If your husband showed up tomorrow would you be ready for him? Have you made room in your house for him? Do you have enough closet and drawer space?" She continued, "Oftentimes, women are consumed with attracting a man and they have not made room for him in their life. If you want the universe to send you something, it is important to practice faith and prepare for the thing you desire."

In the beginning, it seemed like a chore, but eventually the assignment grew on me and I felt excited thinking about the qualities I wanted in a man. It felt like I was giving him life and calling him into existence with my written words. The exercise was powerful. The feeling that my future husband was an idea or dream disappeared and suddenly he seemed real and the sense of urgency to find him dissipated. I felt less pressure to focus on finding a man and instead shifted my attention to doing the inner work to improve my personal and spiritual growth.

Identifying one-hundred and five qualities was not as easy as I thought. Sure, determining the first twenty-five was easy. Then, after a while, it became difficult to identify positive traits. I wondered if part of the assignment was for me to identify the characteristics I needed to develop.

I decided to surrender and submit to the idea that maybe God wanted to use me as a single woman. Maybe a husband would distract me from my calling. Maybe I could reach more people if I were single and did not have to split my time between service and marriage. I submitted to the revelation that God knew best and I did not need to interfere with His plan for my life. On that day, I decided my quest to find a husband was over. I made a renewed commitment to serve God and offered myself up for Him to use me as He saw fit. I can recall this moment in time as if it were yesterday. I remember the date I surrendered because it was the day before God introduced me to *Courage*.

An Encounter with Courage

Being in relationship with God means that He will use every opportunity, situation, circumstance, and encounter to grow your faith in response to your prayers. You can expect God to deliver on His promises in His perfect timing without exceptions. Your faith grows or shrinks based on your thoughts and your thoughts shape your life experiences.

At the time, I was working for a major corporation in Syracuse, considered one of the five largest manufacturing employers in Central New York in the nineties. When the economy shifted, so did the jobs. Many of the plants closed and jobs were shipped overseas to reduce costs. Thus, it was not a surprise when we learned the company was going to merge with a joint venture. At the time of the announcement, I had been working at the corporation for seven years. I was considered a newbie compared to many of my colleagues who had been with the company for fifteen years or more. Unlike my co-workers, I felt hopeful about the merger and the possibility of something new. When my manager asked if I preferred to stay with the old company or transfer with the joint venture, I jumped at the opportunity to transfer. I didn't hesitate because I already knew what to expect with my current employer. I knew my role, the management team, our customers, and how we typically did business. But I didn't know what God had in store for me at the new corporation. And while the future was unknown, I was excited about the endless opportunities God would create.

I wasn't thinking about my employment or job security. I wasn't concerned about the years I had vested with the company or retirement benefits. I was inspired and reenergized by the unlimited possibilities that would come with the merger—new co-workers, new location, and new people. For a second, I thought, *Wouldn't it be interesting if my future husband worked at the new site?* With God, all things are possible, right?

To be in relationship with God is not something that you turn on and off at will. It is a courageous choice to consistently listen, obey, trust, and rely on God to direct your steps. To be in relationship with God is a lifestyle choice. It is the epitome of all relationships. It is the purpose for your Divine Invitations, the reasons why God creates circumstances in your life that force you to grow closer and deepen your relationship with Him. In those moments of desperation, despair, and isolation, you make a conscious choice to cry out to God and forego drugs, alcohol, sex, food, shopping, and gambling because you have faith that God is at the center of your circumstances. Having a relationship with God does not mean that you don't have suicidal or homicidal thoughts. It means that you don't act on those thoughts because you trust with everything in your being that God is going to turn your situation around. In critical times of hurt and confusion, God will set it up so that you know it was Him that brought you through. To be in relationship with God requires a daily practice of forgiveness, passion, unconditional love, honesty, trust, faith, and courage. You may believe there is a God or Higher Power operating in the universe. You may attend church, a mosque, or other religious institutions. You may read the Bible, Quran, or other religious texts. You may pray, fast, meditate, tithe, sing in a choir, feed the homeless, visit the sick and shut in, donate to local charities, serve on nonprofit boards, advocate for vulnerable populations, and otherwise volunteer your time. However, none of that matters if you don't have a personal relationship with the God of your own understanding. I read in one of my devotional journals that, "Religion was designed to size you up, fix you up, and bind you up. Relationship with God, on the other hand, lifts you up and sets you free." Your personal relationship with God makes you free to answer the call, unlock your gifts, and deliver your unique purpose to the world in service to humanity.

One afternoon, I was at work and had a sudden urge for a granola bar. The urge intensified to the point where I heard God whisper, *Now would be a good time to take a break.* Following God's prompt, I decided to go to the vending machine. As I exited the café, I noticed a handsome man talking on the phone with a caramel-pecan tan hue. He was about 5'9" and had a slender build with broad shoulders. He had a contagious smile and a Southern comfort voice. He was definitely eye candy, the only Black person, I had seen on site. We made eye contact before I walked away. For a brief second, I paused, thinking I'd heard him speak to me, but it was obvious he was on the phone.

I decided to take a break outside in the designated employee area and enjoy the warm sun. I suppose Mr. Caramel-Pecan Tan was on a break too because he also wandered outside and sat across from me at the table while he talked on the phone. I didn't want to be rude, so I remained seated and tried to enjoy what was left of my granola bar. After he ended his phone call, we had a nice conversation.

He was a sheet metal foreman that worked for one of the companies in the business complex. He was the first Black person I'd met on campus and I was glad to meet him. He was charming; I enjoyed talking with him. Just before I was about to leave, he asked if he could call me so we could make plans to have lunch together. I gave him my work number, unaware that God had just introduced me to Courage!

When you learn to practice courage because of your trust in God, you begin to speak life into your situations. You begin to think and act confidently. You talk differently. When you have courage because of your absolute faith and trust in God, you can prophesize over your own life and bear witness to His blessings as he intercedes on your behalf.

The next morning, I had a photoshoot scheduled. I was taking professional pictures for an assignment at Inner Visions and I wanted to do something creative—I wanted to look like an angel. The faculty at Inner Visions dressed in all white during classes and we were encouraged to wear white or light colors as well. I wore a white headwrap, sheer shirt with a white tank top underneath, and a broomstick skirt. To complete my ensemble, I wore silver accessories. After the photo shoot, I went to my niece's house to parade around as Mother Theresa so someone else besides the photographer could see how angelic I looked.

When my niece opened the door she said, "Wow, who are you about to marry?"

Jokingly, I said, "Courage. He's in the car and I want you to meet him."

She flung the door open and yelled, "Hey y'all, Dena said she's getting married today."

Taking cues from my smirk, she opted to play along. She grabbed her phone, walked outside and took pictures of me parading around, and then the charade ended.

Surprisingly, I didn't hear from Courage after our conversation. He never called and it seemed liked he vanished from the campus. On walks to the restroom and cafeteria, I hoped to bump into him or at least get a glimpse of him just to know he was still around. It was two months before we reconnected.

What was a girl supposed to think? Under normal circumstances, I would assume I'd said or done something to disinterest him. I remember emailing my girlfriend after I met Courage to let her know I met a handsome, intelligent Black man at work on the day that I happened to look a hot mess. My hair was due for a trim and my jeans were too small. Maybe he felt like I was not interested in him because I gave him my work number instead of my personal cell. In the past, I would have been consumed with "what ifs," but, if you recall, I had just surrendered to God for Him to use me as a single woman.

Two days after my graduation from Inner Visions, I bumped into Courage at work. We were excited to see each other. He was still sporting that contagious smile with beautiful white teeth. He said he'd lost my phone number the same day I gave it to him, and he could not remember my name. He asked several people that worked in my department about me, but no one would give him any information. My co-workers never mentioned that a smooth debonair man was looking for me. He said he wanted to send me flowers, but he couldn't without knowing my name. This time around, I hurried to give him my personal number. He said he would call me after work. Somehow, I missed his call and returned it after ten that night. It seemed like something greater than our understanding was delaying our conversation because we kept missing each other. Nevertheless, we finally scheduled a lunch date. Considering he only had a thirty-minute break, I suggested we walk around the campus for lunch. He agreed and our first date was set.

Courage and I walked and talked. The weather was gorgeous and our pace was steady. I was becoming more attracted to him as he discussed his trade, children, and family. We must have walked three laps around campus before he dropped a bombshell. He was separated from his wife. He did not say it explicitly, but I could read between the lines. At first, I was in denial. I knew he said he was married and had recently moved into his own apartment, but I never heard him mention a divorce. Afraid to learn the truth, I refused to ask. I wanted to relish in the present moment and play with the idea that Courage could potentially be my next boyfriend before I inquired about his marital status.

We went on a few more dates before I asked, "Are you still married?" He told me that he was legally separated. My heart sank and the truth set in. I was entertaining a relationship with a married man. God must have a sense of humor. He connected me with a married man two days after I graduated from a two-year personal development training program. This must be a test, I thought. Maybe God wants Courage to be my first client. Maybe I am supposed to practice my newly developed life coaching skills with Courage to help him get through his divorce. Maybe we are just supposed to be friends despite how attracted I was to him. *Really, God?* Confused about what to do next, I did what any single woman would do—I called my girlfriend for advice.

In her authentic Brooklyn and humorous fashion, she swiftly dismissed my foolish thinking and told me, "Courage don't want you to be his coach, he is trying to get with you."

"Stop playin'!"

Knowing she was right, I felt stuck. I became engrossed by fear and vicious thoughts.

I don't date married men.

I will not be the reason Courage doesn't attempt to reconcile his marriage.

What if I was married and my husband and I were separated? How would I feel if he dated another woman?

What will other women think of me?

What about my loyalty to women? I vowed to never knowingly date a married man.

My girlfriend helped me process my unsettling feelings of guilt so that I could practice courage in what I hoped would become a promising relationship.

Being with Courage felt special. For the first time, I felt fully present in an intimate relationship with a man. Every day, I tried to make sense of my feelings, which were usually "good," so to speak; and then there were other feelings—actually, judgments—that caused me to question my "good" feelings. Doubt crept in. My inner critic asked, *Is this real? What does the future hold for you? The way you're going about this relationship is completely different than how you went about your previous ones, and it's not safe or familiar. Are you sure you know what you're doing?* There was a pattern of self-doubt that surfaced when I acknowledged how happy I was with Courage.

I was stepping out with faith and confronting all self-imposed limitations I had about dating and being intimate with men. Currently, as I write this reflection, I am reminded of how my heart and mind were open to receive love in every possible way.

When I considered the spiritual classroom of my relationship with Courage, I knew God was using him to help me heal my relationship with my father. I recognized I was trying to please Courage in the same way I wanted to please my dad. I didn't want to disappoint Courage or let him down. I wanted to impress him, and I wanted him to be proud of me, but I also wanted him to accept me for me. At times, I felt insecure and afraid to speak my truth, express my concerns, or reveal my judgments. I was afraid to get clarity on the future of our relationship. I was afraid to do or say anything that would potentially rock the boat, for fear of being rejected. I knew my spiritual growth would come from moving through the imagined fears I'd created. The beauty of my relationship with Courage was that every time I started to accept my inner critic's theory for my relationship, he would always do something to contradict it. Oftentimes, he would call or send a text message just when I was battling with a lie—that I am not worthy of love. In an instant, I was reminded of my relationship with God and how God gifted me with Courage for the present moment. Nothing else mattered. I learned to accept the uncertainty of the future. I enjoyed my relationship with Courage and how it made me feel—accepted, desired, appreciated, loved, and supported. For years, I longed to connect with a King who would mirror the true feelings of myself. Courage was my Divine mate.

Although I enjoyed my new experiences with Courage, I could not ignore the internal angst I felt about his marital status. A part of me felt awful for interfering with someone's marriage. Even though they were legally separated, I could not stop thinking about it. I felt compassion for his wife. The old me would have walked away and told Courage to find me after his divorce was finalized. But the spiritual lesson of courage was underway and I needed to flex my spiritual muscles and trust the Divine process as it unfolded.

Sometimes, I felt more challenged with inner turmoil than usual. One day we stopped by Courage's brother's house to pick up something and he asked me to wait in the car because he thought his sister-in-law, a devout Christian, would feel uncomfortable meeting me while he was still married. Another time, Courage did not attend an event with me because his father-in-law was known to frequent the same venue. To make matters even worse, we seldom went out in public because he did not want to parade around town and embarrass his wife. It was hard for me not to feel like the other woman. Despite my feelings, I knew deep down that Courage was being respectful of his estranged wife. Even though he was adamant that reconciliation was not possible, he was cautious not to flaunt our budding relationship in her face out of respect for her and her family. While this did not make me feel any better about our situation, I admired his thoughtfulness and consideration.

This Ain't Funny

In the first six months of my relationship with Courage, I thought God was a prankster. First, He introduced me to Courage, and after I gave him my number, I didn't hear from him for two months.

Second, I learned that Courage was married and the thought of dating him conflicted with my values. I mean, how could I just complete a personal development training program and immediately consider the drama associated with being a third wheel in a relationship?

Third, I discovered Courage was the same man I tried to coach my friend to ask on a date several months before we met. I had to check with my friend and get her blessing.

Fourth, my girlfriend agreed to be my "relationship coach" because I needed support in dating a married man. Go figure! Who on God's green earth solicits a relationship coach to date a married man?

Fifth, God set me up to sit at a table directly across from Courage's wife at a meeting and listen to her share a personal story about loss. As if that was not enough, at the end of the meeting, I was assigned to assist her at a local women's conference.

Sixth, Courage and I took a road trip to Washington, DC, and it is true when they say a road trip will make or break a relationship. My feelings grew immensely during the trip and I recognized I was in love with him.

Seventh, shortly after our trip to DC, Courage decided to break up with me. He said he was unsure if he could "do this" for the rest of his life and apologized for being intimate with me before reaching his conclusion. I was shocked. I did not see that happening. In trying to rationalize the situation, I assumed Courage sensed my intense feelings for him. I thought that may have pushed him away because he was still trying to resolve his marriage. I really didn't know what it was that made him distance himself, but I respected his decision. Though grateful for his honesty, I was disappointed with myself because I knew the risks associated with dating a married man. I set myself up for disappointment. He was rebounding from a marriage and I was learning to honor my feelings and take courageous acts of faith, and this process was not going to go smoothly.

Even my breakup with Courage felt different. It felt like our relationship was complete and there was a distinction between "complete" versus "ended." In the past when my relationships ended, it always felt premature and I experienced anger and hurt. However, with Courage, those feelings were not present. I felt grateful and encouraged. I felt complete. I was able to bear witness to the experience of listening to my intuition, honoring my feelings, and honestly expressing myself to a man. I valued our heartfelt communication.

Despite our decision to end the relationship and go our separate ways was unexpected, I understood. I was able to peacefully reach a mutual agreement with a man who I truly adored. I felt some remorse because I decided not to take the "let's be friends" approach. Past experiences have taught me that approach was unhealthy for me immediately after a breakup. I felt empowered because I was able to honor my need for closure and express my true feelings. In the short period of time that we'd dated I experienced many "firsts" with him. I learned how to be myself and not pretend I was more or less than the real me. I asked for what I wanted. I laughed until it healed. I was open to give and receive love without judgment. I learned that, when I honor who I am and honestly communicate my feelings, rejection is impossible and inner peace is my reward.

After our breakup, it became more evident that Courage was an honorable man. Before we split, he volunteered to weatherize my windows and doors in preparation for the winter. I lived in an older home and there was a cool draft that invaded my house during the winter months. He discussed sealing my windows and doors to prevent the drafts and followed through with his commitment after we parted ways. I didn't expect him to, nor did I ask him. I had forgotten about it. He contacted me and said he wanted to follow through on his promise so that the kids and I could enjoy a warmer home and save money on my gas and electric bill. How thoughtful right? In the back of my mind I was singing, *Whatta man, whatta man, whatta mighty good man!*

As if weatherizing my home weren't enough, Courage continued with more acts of kindness, convincing me that Santa Claus was real. A couple months later he called me on Christmas Eve to see if I was home. I told him I was, and he said he had a couple of gifts for my kids. In about an hour, his daughter knocked on my door and handed me three neatly wrapped packages. I hugged and thanked her for the gifts and waved to Courage as he waited inside his truck. It was thoughtful of him to think about us for Christmas. I had no idea that he was going to buy us gifts. Aside from a text on Thanksgiving Day we had not communicated, and I didn't get him a gift. His consideration of us on Christmas made me feel blessed to have dated him even if it was short-lived. Interestingly, my children weren't even aware that we had stopped dating.

On New Year's Eve, I texted Courage *Happy New Year.* He called me and said he was traveling to visit his family. I told him I was bringing in the New Year at home dancing and eating pizza with the little people—my one-year old great-nieces and nephew. Conversing with him felt good, just like old times. I didn't want the conversation to end, but I needed to finish prepping for the evening. He said he'd call me later in the week, which I thought was a nice gesture.

Courage called me as he said he would. You may be wondering, if he was such an honorable man, why did I not expect him to call? Everything about my relationship with Courage was different—our first encounter, our first date, traveling together, the breakup, and the friendly communication. When we broke up, we weren't mad or upset and there wasn't any hostility. I was not used to that. I was used to having a long, drawn-out breakup filled with sadness and a burning desire to make my ex suffer. I didn't experience that with Courage. I expected there to be some kind of blow-up, and I didn't expect him to call. Thankfully, I was wrong. He did call, and he invited me out for dinner and a movie.

A Turn of Events

Courage and I started going out more. We went to dinner, the movies, social events. Our co-workers could sense that we were dating and seemed happy for us. I met a few of his employees and they raved about how great he was. Things were looking up for us. Courage got divorced and our relationship blossomed even more. We started doing more activities with our children. We split our time between both families for the holidays. We were a committed couple for about six years. During that time, I often wondered if Courage was "the one." He was everything I wanted and so much more. My family loved him and he loved my family. We were great together, but there was one thing that created uncertainty for our future—I wanted to move to Charlotte in a few years and he was not interested in moving. That was a major dilemma for me because I was so focused on the future. I did my best to live in the moment, but one of my character flaws is that I focus on the future to my own detriment. Once, I was so focused on the future, I prematurely grieved the loss of my relationship with Courage because I believed when it came time for him to make a decision about moving, he would choose to stay in Syracuse. I cried like a baby for about five minutes as if we had separated.

There were other times when I found myself overly consumed with the future, separation, and loss. To relieve myself of this perpetual anxiety, I prayed to God and asked, *How will I know my husband*? Suddenly, I remembered when God revealed to me many, many years ago, during one of my meditations, that He was preparing my husband for me. He said, *just like I am preparing you, I am preparing your husband for you.* God told me, *You will know your husband because he will propose to you.* I've had a couple of men discuss marriage with me, but neither proposed. Forgiveness gave me two rings. Once when we were shopping in NYC for school clothes for the kids, we stopped by a jewelry store. I tried on a beautiful diamond ring and he asked me if I wanted it. I said *yes* and he bought it. I believe he gave me the first ring as a promise to buy a more expensive ring in the future. In both cases, he never asked me to marry him. Unconditional Love contemplated getting me a ring from the pawn shop and I told him that was not a good idea because of the potential history associated with it.

More time lapsed and, in another prayer, I asked God a clarifying question: *How will I recognize the husband You've prepared for me*? God responded, *You will know the husband I have prepared for you because he will ask your father for your hand in marriage.* I heard God's answer and felt uncomfortable because I thought this was the one time God was going to be wrong. There was no way, in the twenty-first century, that an older man was going to ask my father for my hand in marriage, especially since I was grown, lived on my own, and had children already. Now, God could be sending a young whippersnapper my way, but I doubted that too. And I certainly didn't think Courage would do it. We were older—he was in his mid-forties and I was almost forty—so I doubted God's answer and continued to wonder if Courage was the one. I thought about what my next steps should be if he was not. Should we continue dating? Should we separate? Should we become business partners?

Forty and Focused

I love the month of October because it signifies a new year for me. My new year begins on my birthday—October 7th—not on January 1st. Each October, I get enthused about setting new goals and expectations for myself and the year ahead. I seek opportunities and strategies to improve and expand my relationship with God. I expect to be refined every year. This new year was monumental—I was turning forty. My mantra was, *I am forty and focused!* I was ecstatic about God's plan for me in this new decade. I'd finally graduated from my thirties and turned a new leaf. I was living a courageous life with an incredible support system and could not wait to see what God revealed next. I had great expectations for my new season in life.

For my birthday, I chose to celebrate with family and friends at a Brazilian Steakhouse. We had an amazing dinner and it was the first time some of my close friends from my childhood got to meet Courage. Everyone had a great time. We laughed and reminisced about the good ole days in between stuffing our mouths with scrumptious steak, lamb, chicken, and sausage. Later that evening, we danced off the excess calories to the tunes of a live band.

A couple of weeks after the start of my new year I started to get that itch again—I started consuming myself with thoughts about where my relationship with Courage was heading, moving to Charlotte, and separation. I started to feel agitated to the point that I wanted 'a talk' with Courage about our future. My Friday morning didn't get off to a good start. I got caught in the rain, I left my lunch at home, and I felt upset for no apparent reason. Fired up, I was convinced that I needed to have the talk with Courage after work. I wanted to sit down with him and put everything on the table. Whatever we decided, I wanted us to be honest about our desires and plan accordingly. Unexpectedly, Courage came home late, and I decided to postpone the conversation until the next day.

On Saturday we had a lot of errands to run. We were going to a formal event later in the evening, and I had to buy a dress, get a manicure and pedicure, and take my mom across town to visit her nephew. I planned to talk with Courage either on the drive to the event or on our way home.

The Conversation

Courage and I were finally dressed and ready to leave. Running late was our norm, but this time we were really determined to be on time because we were meeting his brother and sister-in-law. My plan was to initiate the conversation in the car, but Courage decided to stop by my parent's apartment. I tried to convince him to stop by after, but he insisted we do it while we still looked impeccable.

We walked up three flights of stairs to their apartment which, helped me break in my brand new, four-inch heels. The lights in the apartment were off, but I could hear the television playing in the bedroom. I yelled, "Hello," and my father invited us back to his room. He was home alone, and my mother was still out visiting with her nephew. We modeled for a quick second, and I stopped to check myself in the full-length door mirror. I heard Courage telling my dad he wanted to introduce me as his fiancé tonight. I thought that was kind of strange because I wasn't his fiancé. Somewhat perplexed, I couldn't figure out why Courage was bringing that up now. I continued to admire myself in the mirror and Courage continued his conversation.

He said, "I love your daughter and I would like to ask your permission for her hand in marriage."

Now I was really confused.

I turned to look at them and my father yelled, "Yes!"

Then Courage turned to me, pulled a small green ring box out of his pocket, dropped to one knee, and asked me if I would marry him.

In disbelief, I said, "YES!"

I grabbed Courage by the cheeks and kissed him several times. He stood up, we embraced, and I started yelling, *I'm a fiancé! I'm a fiancé!*

We planned our wedding in nine months. We set the date, selected the color scheme, chose the venue, picked our wedding party, determined the budget, and created a savings plan to support the vision. Things progressed rather quickly. Courage and I had been together for over six years and we knew we wanted to spend the rest of our lives together. After his proposal, I knew that was God's plan for us as well. I finally received confirmation that Courage was the one. I was fully aware that he was the man God had prepared for me. All uncertainty, doubt, and questions about the future of our relationship disappeared. I felt an overwhelming sense of peace about my future. Relocating to Charlotte no longer seemed important. Buying another house did not matter. What was on the horizon was planning our wedding and spending the rest of our lives together as husband and wife.

Now that it was clear that we were getting married we decided to forego a long engagement period. Considering my parents' health, we wanted to have the ceremony as soon as feasible. I wanted my father to walk me down the aisle. I wanted my mother to see her "baby" get married. I wanted my parents to witness God's miraculous work in uniting Courage and I as one, in holy matrimony, in the presence of close friends and family. Every time I thought about my eighty-year-old father walking me down the aisle, I would get excited. The thought of marching down the aisle with my dad made me marvel at the goodness of God.

Courage and I experienced significant challenges with our parents' health. His dad suffered a stroke and died a year after we started dating. His mom developed brain cancer and battled her illness for eighteen months. Although, I did not have an opportunity to meet Courage's father before he passed, his mom and I became close in the five years before she passed. In her final hours, as she lay in a hospital bed in her living room after suffering a seizure, I made her a promise. It was just the two of us; I held her hand and vowed to love, honor, and respect Courage to the best of my ability. I told her to not worry about him—I would love him and take care of him and make her proud of me. I told her she raised an honorable man and that I would not disappoint her. I would ensure that his needs were met. Four hours later, she passed. As sad as it was, I felt a sense of peace having had that final conversation before her transition.

My mother's dementia advanced after my father had open heart surgery in 2015, and it felt like we were in chronic crisis because of the unpredictability of their health. My mom started falling more frequently, my father got sick when he missed dialysis, and their sporadic hospitalizations left us on edge. It definitely wreaked havoc on my nerves, while we were trying to do everything we could to prevent falls and keep them safe.

Initially, planning the wedding seemed effortless. I had thought about it most of my adult life and knew what I wanted—something small, intimate, and spiritual. I wanted the presence of God to be felt at the ceremony. I only wanted close family and friends to attend. I wanted to honor our parents and demonstrate to God that we were serious about our commitment to marriage. I wanted our guests to leave inspired, with a renewed interest in their personal relationship with God. I wanted a ceremony that reflected my spirituality.

Our wedding party was small. It consisted of my best friend, my sister-in-law, our children, Courage's brother and his two best friends. My former relationship coach was the wedding coordinator, and other friends volunteered, at my request, to help on the day of the wedding.

With all wedding planning, you are guaranteed to have some hiccups. And you can bet your honeymoon that you will get frustrated, and some family members will be upset with you after the wedding party is selected. This was true for me, and in those moments of agitation, I reminded myself that the only people required to show up at the wedding was me, Courage, and the pastor. Everyone else was extra. I won't harp on the hitches because they were really minor in the grand scheme of things. Ninety percent of the planning was without incident, and in my times of craziness, Courage talked me down. I would however, like to highlight three memorable events leading up to the wedding: our engagement dinner, my bridal shower, and my spiritualette party, all of which made me a very gracious bride-to-be.

My best friend of more than thirty years hosted our engagement dinner. I'm sure you're thinking that's not a big deal—that's what best friends are supposed to do, right? Well that would have been true if she wasn't going through a divorce. She had been married for eighteen years and the plan was for her and her husband to stand at the altar with me on my wedding day. When she mentioned they were considering divorce I felt discouraged. Not because of my wish for them to be at the altar, but because their marriage represented my ideal vision of love, support, and partnership. The thoughtfulness, excitement, and selflessness that my best friend showed while coordinating and hosting my engagement party was a sheer act of unconditional love and support. After her marriage ended with someone I considered her knight and shining armor, she had every right to be bitter, angry, and emotionally unavailable to support me in my upcoming wedding. I was astonished at how gracefully she managed the dissolution of her marriage. I admired her strength as she tackled every twist and turn that arose from separation, loss of income, and co-parenting. My best friend has always been there for me for every milestone, including the birth of my children, leaving my abuser, purchasing my first home, my children's graduations, and their journeys to college. However, this time life was taking her through the ringer, and, despite every obstacle she faced, she encouraged and supported me and my bridal activities. To have her support meant the world to me.

My bridal shower was held a month before my wedding at my best friend's house, and my sister-in-law helped coordinate it. We had a wonderful time filled with fun, food, fellowship, and laughter. We played games, and many of the ladies shared stories of their first encounters with Courage and me. It was refreshing. I felt overjoyed at their outpouring of love and encouragement. Before we dispersed for the evening, Courage's mother's best friend pulled me aside and told me that "mom" would be pleased with me and she was happy about our union. It was a powerful confirmation and it warmed my heart.

The morning after my bridal shower, I was sitting in my car in the parking lot at the grocery store reviewing pictures and text messages, when I experienced a sudden rush of emotion. Reliving the events from my bridal shower, I burst into tears of appreciation. I felt sheer gratitude for each woman that decided to take time out of their busy schedule to attend. Their presence was more than enough and their gifts were the icing on the cake. Vividly, I recalled each time the doorbell rang, and I opened it. Each woman that entered was going through some kind of personal struggle, whether it was related to health, finances, unemployment, heartbreak, divorce, depression, recovery from a surgery, struggling with young children, family dysfunction, or driving one-hundred and fifty miles to be there. I thought about their struggles, remembered their encouraging words and gifts and I just sobbed. I could not stop crying tears of gratitude. I could not catch my breath. The amazing women I often refer to as sister girlfriends left a profound impression on my heart and soul. For them and their generous acts of kindness I am forever grateful.

As you should know by now, I am a spiritual being governed by the Holy Spirit that dwells within. I move to the tune of my own beat and most of the time, I do not concern myself with what others think about me. I have learned that people will always have an opinion of you. There was a time when I desired to please people. I wanted to be liked and consumed myself with other people's opinions of me. Fortunately, I grew spiritually and learned the most important opinion was that of God. God is my judge, not man, and I aspire to follow the inner promptings of the Holy Spirit. Thus, it should not come as a surprise that I decided to forego the traditional bachelorette party for a "spiritualette" party.

That's right, I created a new nomenclature to support my future role as a wife. A role I regarded with high esteem. Contrary to traditional bachelorette parties—spending an evening out clubbing, dancing, and watching strippers—I wanted to be in the company of wise women who would pray, uplift, encourage, and affirm my new role as a wife. I wanted a safe space where I could worship, shout, cry, and be comforted when the insecurities and anxieties surfaced. I wanted to connect with women of faith and feel their heartfelt prayers for my union while encircled in prayer. I wanted to feel the presence of the Holy Spirit as I gathered with select women who knew how to be wives and mothers and lead purpose-driven lives. There was only one woman who could pull off my vision for the spiritualette party, and that was my sister-in-law, a phenomenal woman, wife, mother, and missionary. She had been praying for our union for years and it was only right that she hosted this special event.

The spiritualette party was more than what I envisioned. My sister-in-law took my request before God. She prayed and consulted with the First Lady of our church and other missionaries for counsel and guidance, and she delivered. It was incredible to see how she took my idea and made it a reality. This was also the first bridal event that my mother attended. She was reenergized by the personal testimonies and prayer. She smiled and nodded as different speakers shared. Some women presented inspirational gifts, poems, and scriptures. Some talked about their journeys to partnering with their husbands and supporting them in sickness and in health. One of the mothers from our church spoke about being married to a preacher for over thirty years. I could not have asked for a better event. To top it off, my sister-in-law said that organizing the spiritualette party inspired her to start her own business, a ministry for women. To God be the glory!

Many women dream of marrying their prince charming. We hope that prince charming will show up on our doorstep one day and whisk us away in a horse and carriage. If we believed that this would really happen, we would certainly want to prepare for it. Preparation is key to readying yourself for marriage. God prepared me through Inner Visions for the day that I would meet my husband. And God prepared my husband for when he would meet me. Because of this, I was intentional about preparing for our union so that when trials and tribulations threatened our communication I would be armed and ready with spiritual weapons and tools. It also helped that my sister-in-law gifted me the book, *The Power of a Praying Wife,* and we studied it together.

The Ceremony

On July 29, 2017, I married my Divine mate, friend, confidant, cheerleader, supporter, provider, protector, and personal King. It was a special day filled with love, laughter, and the Holy Spirit. My daughter was my right hand. She put the finishing touches on favors and reassured me that she had my back on any last-minute errands. My wedding coordinator worked tirelessly to ensure the ceremony and reception went off successfully; if there were any issues, she made sure I did not know about them.

The ceremony took place at three in the afternoon. The temperature was in the high eighties and the sun's rays beamed on the formal white chairs that lined the grassy backyard of the Wysockis Manor in Cicero. The scenery was perfect, better than I had imagined. I wanted an outdoor wedding so that we would be connected to God and nature.

Family and friends were escorted to their seats by my nephews while the musician played the cello. Courage's niece initiated the ceremony with a liturgical dance to the song, "Grateful," by Hezekiah Walker. "Grateful" is my favorite gospel song because it depicts my gratitude for my relationship with God, the mercy He shows me, and the bountiful blessings He bestows upon me. Grateful is how I feel on any given day. Weeks before my wedding day, I had a revelation that God was partnering me with a man with whom God expects me to do great things with for His glory. Our partnership will allow us to minister to God's people for a purpose yet to be revealed. God has a mighty plan for us and I look forward to doing His will.

My parents, siblings, nieces, nephews, cousins, friends, and soon to be in-laws looked on as we prepared to exchange vows. I felt their love and support and my heart was overwhelmed with joy and gratitude. My great-niece, the flower girl, was emotional as well. I later learned she cried tears of joy at the altar. Before Courage and I took our vows, my god-niece sung "Angel of Mine," by Monica, which I dedicated to Courage. With the exception of the artist, no one was more suited for the soloist role at my wedding. My god-niece is a powerful, afro-centric young woman rooted in confidence beyond her years. She witnessed the evolution of my journey from being a single mother, to dating Unconditional Love, to finding love and happiness with Courage.

We exchanged traditional vows from the Bible. We considered writing our own, and then Courage reminded me of the additional stress that would result from having to remember and recite personal vows. He said there was no need to add unnecessary stress. I told you he is great—he is always helping me find ways to manage my load and lighten it whenever possible, which is one reason I said *yes* to partnering with him for life. He helps me maintain balance.

Our wedding bands were simple gold bands. You may have assumed that, because of my God-driven aspirations and goals, lofty ideas for entrepreneurship, and relentless desire to have an extravagant brick house with a staff to maintain it, I would want a jaw-dropping, eye-catching, jeweled wedding band. And yet I did not. At least not anymore.

In my unhealed state of mind, just after my relationship with Forgiveness ended, I was infatuated with the idea of having an expensive wedding ring. The ring symbolized security and insurance to protect my personal investment of time and money should my next relationship fail. I expected a man to give me a ring valued at twenty-five thousand dollars or more. In those days, I didn't consider marriage a ministry. I didn't think love was necessary. I focused on the contractual obligations and thought of marriage as a business transaction. But to God be the glory. Inner Visions helped me to heal that mindset, practice forgiveness, and appreciate all the lessons learned along the way. Courage could have proposed with a plastic ring out of the vending machine and it would not have mattered because I knew he was sent from God.

After we exchanged rings, we lit a unity candle in honor of Courage's deceased parents. I remember praying that my veil did not catch fire while I tried to light the candle. In retrospect, I am pleased that I planned a spirit-filled ceremony because I certainly did a lot of praying during my final moments as a single woman.

Mr. and Mrs. Garner

We knew we were a special couple when the pastor told us to redo our first kiss.

He said, "Wait a minute now, y'all gave me this schedule that had timing for everything including a two-minute kiss. That kiss didn't look like it was two minutes. I think y'all should redo that."

I was officially a Mrs., graced with a new outlook on life. Not in an arrogant way, but with confidence. From this moment forward we would be doing this thing called life together. Win, lose, or draw, we were partners. We were aware that life would not always be as sweet as pie, but we expected to have way more sweetness than not.

We had a wonderful time at the reception. We laughed, danced, and celebrated our union. Music and dancing were an essential part of the reception. Dancing is my favorite sport and music helps to set the atmosphere. I pre-selected nearly every song the DJ played to help set the mood during certain activities of the reception.

Some folks cautioned that after all the preparation, anxiety, and frustration that goes into planning the big day, I probably wouldn't remember the wedding. Thankfully, that was not my experience. Maybe it's because I was not under the influence of alcohol, or maybe God gave me a supernatural ability to remember details so I could recall them for this book. Or maybe my frustration and anxiety were so low that by the time the day arrived I was at baseline. Whatever the reason, I am glad for my memories. Planning that day was a huge project that required lots of coordination, time, prayers, and support. I am grateful to all my family and friends who contributed in their special way.

The Spiritual Lesson of Courage

Courage is not exercised until you come face to face with a perceived threat and are forced to make a decision that requires trust and faith. When that opportunity is presented, life will demand that you practice courage.

About a month before our first wedding anniversary, my world flipped upside down. My safety net dissipated, my sense of security vanished, my relationship with God tested, and my trust, faith and confidence in myself and my marriage were hanging by a thread. Under no circumstances could I have imagined getting pregnant at forty-one after being on birth control pills for over sixteen years. I was devastated. Sitting in the bathroom staring at the results of the home pregnancy test, I thought it had to be wrong. This couldn't be real. But the word PREGNANT was crystal clear on the digital display. There was no room for misinterpretation.

I'd actually taken the test to rule out pregnancy. I'd lost five pounds after completing a three-day green smoothie detox, but then I noticed that four pounds returned just one day after I stopped it. I also hadn't had a period in over a month. I decided to take the test as a precaution. I never expected to get a positive result.

You would think being in a loving marriage and having a surprise pregnancy was a wonderful blessing from God. Under most circumstances, I would agree. But this was different. God, along with everyone I know, knew I did not want more children. I knew birth control pills were not one-hundred percent effective, but I was confident I was safe. I did not conceive while I was on the pill. There was one month

I had to refill my prescription at a different pharmacy. I filled my prescription in April and assumed I could refill it at the new pharmacy again in May. That assumption proved to be life- altering. The pharmacist said I needed to have my doctor transfer the prescription to have it refilled on a permanent basis. Being lackadaisical about the matter, I didn't take the pill for a month. Conception occurred sometime in May.

The pregnancy triggered all my insecurities, most of which stemmed from childhood. I was deathly afraid of what to do next. In the bathroom, with the test in my hand, I thought about my future with Courage. Whatever I decided to do next, my relationship would be changed forever, and I was conflicted. In most situations I was the optimist. I can immediately find a blessing or spiritual lesson in every situation. Not this time. My fears became dominant and I began to wallow in self-doubt.

I thought about the possibility of raising another child as a single parent. What would happen if Courage decided to leave me? I couldn't handle that. I didn't have the capacity to be a single mother again. I could not fathom going through a divorce and being with a young child in this phase of my life. On top of abandonment issues, I thought about potential rejection. What if I got too big during the pregnancy and Courage found me unattractive? What if we had to stop having sex—would he desire someone else? What if the baby was born with a defect? How would we adjust? How would that impact our relationship? What if Courage fell deeply in love with the newborn and totally forget about my needs for attention and affection? What if, after the baby was born, we were unable to spend quality time together? I did not want to risk losing Courage's love and affection. As a Libra, I long for that—I need attention. A newborn baby would require Courage to divide his time even more and I wanted as much of his love, attention, and time as I could possibly have. Our responsibilities were already stretching us thin, and I didn't want to add an additional strain.

Eventually, I uncovered the root cause of the insecurities—it was my core belief of not being important. Masked underneath the surface fears was a belief that I would lose Courage's love because he would no longer consider me important with a new baby. I was terrified that he would stop loving me and I would be abandoned and rejected again. These thoughts felt very real and unbearable. I anticipated the distress and loss that would occur because of having a baby.

Still standing in the bathroom in front of the mirror, I contemplated my options. I could walk out of the bathroom, ignore the results, and carry on as if nothing were wrong. Maybe it was a false positive.

I could not say anything to Courage and secretly get an abortion. Although this felt like a plausible solution, I did not want to live a lie. Communication is critical in relationships. I valued our relationship too much to destroy it in this way.

I thought about pleading with Courage to agree to an abortion. I figured maybe we could negotiate and I could persuade him to give up the idea of having a baby. In my heart, I knew Courage would never agree to this, and would be offended and hurt.

The last option seemed the least doable. I could walk into my bedroom and tell Courage the truth. Just thinking about the truth had my heart beating irregularly.

For the first time in my relationship with Courage, I could not anticipate a favorable outcome. Whichever option I decided, I was convinced it would destroy my seemingly perfect relationship, and I had to accept that possibility. My faith was about to be tested in an area I was not prepared for.

With the greatest fear before me, I mustered up the courage to exit the bathroom and tell Courage the truth. He didn't believe me at first. Once I told him I would never joke about something this serious he grew excited. Privately, I tried to mask my feelings of self-hate behind a fake smile to allow him the opportunity to have his experience. On the inside, my inner peace was annihilated. It was hard for me to accept that I'd put myself in this irreversible predicament. God had offered me a Divine Invitation to master courage and I was an unwilling participant.

God's Plan

As a spiritual being, it can be difficult for others to accept my beliefs and convictions, and I am empathetic to their lack of understanding. But it is important for me to emphasize my foundational beliefs—God is responsible for *everything* that happens in my life. I give God the credit for all blessings, spiritual lessons, opportunities, mercy, and grace. I believe God is the only source, the greatest source and there is nothing that is comparable to His infinite wisdom and energy. Various religions subscribe to the notion of the devil, Satan, or other evil forces, and I do not. I do not give reverence to anything outside of God, the All Knowing, All Merciful, and Omnipresent.

It is not my desire to convince anyone to change their beliefs. My intent is to spread the gospel based on my personal relationship with God. I practice relationship, not religion. I am confident in my relationship with God and trust His guidance and plans for my life. I do not live life on my own terms, I live life on God's terms, according to the inner promptings of the Holy Spirit present within. Every day, I pray that I do God's will for my life. I choose to develop and maintain my relationship with God for spiritual understanding, knowledge, and wisdom. I can only embody the seven spiritual lessons of relationships because of my personal relationship with God. I don't expect everyone to understand me, but I challenge everyone reading this book to be open to developing and growing a personal relationship with God, the God of your own understanding.

After hearing the baby's heartbeat during my first ultrasound, I knew there was a little baby growing inside my womb. It was surreal. I've had ultrasounds in the past, but I've never heard or seen the baby's heartbeat. I was amazed by the sound of the heartbeat and in awe of the advancements of technology that allowed me to hear it. It just seemed unreal, not because I was fearful, but because of the wondrous act of God that allowed Courage's seed to fertilize my egg to create a tiny human being. According to the ultrasound, I was ten weeks and two days pregnant, and my due date was February 27.

For years I discussed spiritual pregnancies and the work God wanted to birth through me, and now I was carrying a fetus that was forming before my eyes. I started to come to terms with the pregnancy and began seeing the blessings in disguise. This pregnancy was the product of a loving partnership. Unlike the conditions we were in when we first became parents two decades ago, our relationship was solid, our careers established, and our finances secure. We had the best conditions to bring a new bundle of joy into. Once I shared the news with our family and friends and the shock subsided, we saw that we had a lot of support. Our family was thrilled by the news. I was beginning to anticipate this little one being a bridge to bring our families closer. My friends started discussing baby showers, my niece wanted overnights and playdates, my sister-in-law agreed to decorate the nursery and spend weekends with us to help out, and Courage and I were contemplating baby names. If it was a girl, I wanted her name to carry the meaning of *faith*. Courage and I settled on *Imani*, which means "faith" in Swahili. If it was a boy, which I knew Courage really wanted, we agreed to name him after Courage.

We were excited about the many ways in which the baby would bless and enrich our life. Courage prayed nightly over my womb. We wanted the little one to hear his voice and marinate in the vibrational energy of prayer. I told Courage we had to read Rick Warren's *The Purpose Driven Life* to the baby before he or she was born to facilitate their spiritual understanding of what they were born to be and do.

Courage spoiled me even more and made sure the refrigerator was stocked with my favorite grape juice. Our children made peace with the news of welcoming a new sibling in seven months. We were planning to purchase another house to accommodate our growing family. I informed my colleagues and staff that I was expecting.

Support and excitement for the baby continued to grow. This pregnancy was taking an unexpected twist and I felt encouraged every step of the way.

After the ultrasound, our prenatal visit was scheduled for the end of August. I was anxious to meet with my doctor because I knew she would be shocked about the pregnancy as well. I have a great relationship with my doctor. She is also the primary care physician for my children. She understands and respects my views on medicine and educates me on different options and alternatives. She even asks about my entrepreneurial efforts at my annual exams. I think she's terrific. I couldn't wait to introduce her to Courage because I wanted her to meet the man responsible for this surprise pregnancy. We were also eager to hear her medical knowledge for high risk pregnancies.

I had to be diligent about my meetings at work to ensure I left work in enough time to make it to my first prenatal visit. This was the first appointment that Courage and I were attending together. I could tell he was nervous because he texted me several times throughout the day for the address and appointment time. He wanted to make sure he allowed enough travel time to the appointment because he worked an hour away. Fortunately, we both arrived to the doctor's office with plenty of time to spare. We were able to decompress from work and focus on the purpose of the visit.

When I introduced Courage to my doctor, she told him she'd heard great things about him. She explained that she would listen to the baby's heartbeat, discuss the pregnancy and associated risks, and address any questions or concerns we had. I laid on my back and she placed a cold gel on my stomach so she could listen to the baby's heartbeat with the fetal Doppler. The doctor slid the probe back and forth across my stomach in silence and all we could hear on the monitor was static. She moved the probe left and right, up and down for about two minutes before uttering, "My machine could be defective. I'm going to send you down the hall to get another ultrasound because I can't hear the heartbeat."

While I got dressed in silence, a million thoughts ran through my mind, none of which I can recall. Courage and I exited the patient room without saying a word and walked down the hall to the lab. We waited about fifteen minutes before the ultrasound technician examined me. She was young and quiet. She did not give any information or explain her procedure. Courage sat in a chair across from me and the monitor. He could see everything and I could not hear anything. I asked if she saw a heartbeat and she explained that she was just taking photos and the doctor would have to analyze the results. She was unhelpful. If Courage weren't there, I would have been less cooperative and would have requested a new technician.

The technician completed the ultrasound and promised to send the results over to my doctor's office. I wiped the gel off my stomach, pulled the top of my pants up and fastened the button. I asked Courage what he'd seen on the monitor and he said, "I'm not sure, Babe." Something didn't feel right. Courage showed no emotion and I couldn't read him. We walked back to my doctor's office and went into the examination room. The mood was solemn. It seemed like everyone knew what was going on except me. When the doctor returned, she asked how we were doing.

I'm sure the looks on our faces were puzzled, because she followed up with, "Did they tell you the results of the ultrasound?"

I said, "No."

She sighed. "Oh, I'm sorry. I thought they told you. There was no heartbeat. You had a miscarriage and I am so sorry for your loss. Because it is a loss."

"When?" I asked, trying to process this news.

She said it had happened sometime after my tenth week. It was concerning that I hadn't expelled the pregnancy tissue yet. She said that I needed to decide whether I wanted to wait another week to see if I passed the tissue on my own with the aid of medication, which was not guaranteed to work, or if I wanted to have a D&C procedure to remove the tissue from my uterus. She shared her story about her own miscarriage— after taking the medicine, she'd still needed the D&C. Time was of the essence. The longer the tissue remained in my uterus, the greater my risk for getting an infection. She discussed the procedure and the risks with both options and then left the room to give us time to process our loss and make a decision.

I was dumbfounded. I could not rationalize this cruel joke God was playing. I wanted to be strong for Courage. I tried to hold back the tears but with each utterance of, "I don't understand," the tears flowed stronger and stronger, and before I knew it, I was weeping in Courage's arms. He consoled me as best he could.

He said, "We took a loss today, Babe. We'll get through it."

We embraced for a while before we discussed our options. We both agreed that the D&C was the better option and shared that with the doctor. Fortunately, we were able to schedule the procedure for the end of the week. Courage and I left the doctor's office in a daze. It felt like we were in the aftermath of a hurricane, waiting to be rescued. On my drive home I continued to question God. I wanted an immediate answer to rationalize this nightmare. When I got home, I went straight to bed, hoping that when I awoke the next day this terrible dream would be over.

In the days following the news of the miscarriage, I started to unravel emotionally. My self-confidence, self-esteem, and positive self-image diminished. I believed my body had failed me, and I felt ashamed and embarrassed. This was my first miscarriage. I thought I was healthy and yet, I was unable to carry the baby to term. If God wanted me to know what it felt like to miscarry so that I could identify with that population of women, He was successful. It's a terrible feeling that only a woman who has experienced it can relate to. The internal conversations are ruthless on your self-worth. These conversations made me feel more depleted each day. The sad thing was, I did not have time to process my feelings. I took one day off work and then ended up working sixteen hours the next day. I wanted to grieve. I wanted to feel my feelings. I wanted to reflect and pray and meditate. I wanted to take time off from work, but I couldn't because my team was depending on me to facilitate several mandatory trainings. My next day off was for the D&C on Friday.

If there was a time in my life when I needed the Lord to take the wheel it was during my dark days after the miscarriage. I felt conflicted because of my personal relationship with God. I knew He was in control of my situation, and yet, I could not make sense of it. I could not comprehend why He would allow us to conceive only to take it away. It simply blew my mind. I thought if God didn't want us to have a baby then He should not have allowed me to see and hear the baby's heartbeat. Why did He allow me to become attached? Why did He allow me to tell my family and friends? Why did He allow us to conceive when we were not trying to get pregnant? The more I questioned God, the more tormented I became. I felt abandoned by God. He knew I strived to please Him, and I felt like I was being punished. Why else would He allow me to suffer this way?

I blamed myself for the miscarriage. If my thoughts weren't so negative in the beginning, maybe this would not have happened. It was baffling that, for the first time ever, I became excited about my pregnancy. I anticipated the overflow of love, support, and blessings the baby would receive from us and how the baby would enrich our lives. I wanted this baby. And then out of the blue, I miscarry. *Why now, Lord?*

After the D&C I felt more alone and discouraged. Courage stayed with me during the procedure, brought me home, made sure I was comfortable, and bought my favorite salad from Chipotle. Then he left to go to Elmira to pick up his cousins. I'm sure he needed to drive to clear his head, and I wanted the space to be alone with my thoughts. While I had some minor discomfort from the procedure, I was more disturbed by the emotional pain. I wanted to sleep away my feelings of hurt, confusion, disappointment, failure, and unworthiness. But I couldn't escape them. With every physical discomfort I was reminded of the loss of our unborn child and my inner peace. I knew my life and my marriage would never be the same; part of me was dying on the inside and there was nothing I could do to interrupt the process. It had to take its course, no matter how painful it was.

For the next twenty-four hours I suffered in silence because I was not ready to share the loss with others. I didn't want to talk about it. I didn't want to discuss the pain. I didn't want others to notice my weakness and feel sympathy for me. I didn't want to leave the house or be around people. I didn't want anyone to ask me how I was doing or feeling. I wanted to be alone.

In those deep, dark moments, I couldn't write in my journal or read inspirational material. The only thing I could do was watch TV and be with my thoughts. I was depressed. I faked a smile or two so Courage would not be alarmed, but I was experiencing my first round of conscious depression. I had unexpressed self-hate bottling up on the inside and no outlet. Under normal circumstances, I could journal, pray, read a devotional, or talk to someone, but I didn't have the desire or energy to do it. It was going to take a Divine Invitation to get me through this process. Somehow, I mustered up an ounce of hope to remind myself to trust God.

With every negative thought, doubt, and insecurity, I whispered to myself, *Trust God.* Deep within I knew God had a plan for the miscarriage, just like He did with everything else. My thoughts started to shift as I continued to remind myself to trust God. I knew He did not want me to become complacent with my faith and was inviting me to grow exponentially through this experience. Thankfully, God did not allow me to suffer too long before revealing His purpose for the pregnancy. On a September morning, I wrote the following entry in my journal:

Journal you've missed a lot. Two months ago from this date I learned I was pregnant. On July 18, I saw and heard the baby's heartbeat. On August 27, we learned I miscarried and there was no heartbeat. On August 31, I had a D&C procedure to clean my cervix of the missed miscarriage. I've had a lot of emotions pertaining to this pregnancy, my future, my marriage, my dreams and aspirations. I went from feeling disbelief, fear, shame, acceptance, and excitement to disbelief, hurt, sadness, embarrassment, anger, and frustration with God, to confusion, trust, and now peace! I was reading the book Play Your Bigger Game by Rick Tamlyn, (page 42) and he used the analogy playing the bigger game is similar to a pregnancy—you know the pregnancy will change your life, and yet you're unsure how! Well what I learned in reading that was insightful. The question I should be asking is not Lord why did you allow this to happen (victim consciousness) but rather how did this "pregnancy" change my life? Remember I profess and wholeheartedly believe that everything that happens in life has a spiritual nature and there is a lesson or blessing in every situation. My emotions blinded me to this fact and although I continued to trust God in the process. I was baffled and confused because of what I thought was a blow to my self-esteem. When I reflect on how my life has changed because of this pregnancy, I am reminded of the wonderfulness and beauty of God. The changes that have occurred since the pregnancy are:

- I discussed my fears of abandonment/rejection and not being loved with Courage.
- I took my faith to a deeper level—learning to trust and put my faith in man (husband).
- I met with a loan officer and implemented a new savings plan.
- I started preparing my direct reports to lead the program in my absence.
- I had personal conversations with staff (unexpectedly) and made deeper connections.
- I received additional support and compassion from family and friends.
- I connected on a deeper level with my daughter.
- I renewed hope and excitement for the future.
- I reprioritized home improvements and repairs.
- I made a new commitment to reading for self-improvement.
- I increased intimacy in my marriage—we were vulnerable with each other and discussed our insecurities.
- I was willing and open to doing the one thing I said I could NEVER do!
- I practiced love without conditions.
- Courage and I experienced and survived our first loss together.

Lord, I thank you for the healing! I am healed. I overstand. I see the blessing in this experience. I appreciate the pregnancy and what it produced. I am grateful to you God for the continuous lessons and blessings You bestow upon me. This is yet another experience I can add to my repertoire for demonstrating courage. That was the ultimate! I love you Lord. I'm ready to finish the book and complete this assignment. The End!

Journaling is a profound way to document your private conversations with God. When I journal, I'm less focused on my writing style as I am with the messages and revelations I receive from God. My journaling is usually inspired by a situation or event that I need to process emotionally. Using pen and paper helps a great deal. Based on the above journal entry, one would assume the pregnancy chapter was closed, right? Wrong. God still had plans to use this situation for His glory.

The day after I experienced my healing, Courage said, "We need to talk," which took me by surprise. He told me that he wanted another baby and he wanted to try again. Until this point, he'd never declared his desire for more children. When asked if he wanted more kids, his typical response was, "I'm not sure." Unlike me, Courage seldom professed what he wanted, so whenever he said, "I want..." I found it sexy and attractive. However, in this situation, I was scared and did not want to try again. I didn't think I could emotionally handle another miscarriage. Quite honestly, I was pissed that he even wanted to try again. Especially after everything I'd just gone through. Why would he even consider trying to conceive again?

I was in my head, dealing with my own thoughts and concerns, while he was explaining his rationale. Then suddenly, it dawned on me. The week before I had been processing and going through my own healing process, and now he was going through his. Immediately, I became open and present, attentively listening to Courage as he expressed his longing for a baby. Eventually the conversation came to a halt and he asked for some ice cream and a glass of water. When I went downstairs to get it, God spoke to me. He said:

I'm teaching you to trust man—your husband. You trust Me, now it's time to grow your faith and trust and connect with your husband. The first step was having the courage to do the one thing you said you could never do. Now that you and your husband have agreed to pray about the situation [to have another baby], you have to trust that as the head, he will listen to Divine guidance and lead you in the right direction.

God is certainly in the business of transformation and constant spiritual growth. I must have coasted long enough to warrant these rapid Divine Invitations. Since the beginning of my spiritual walk, I've had the faith of a mustard seed and then it grew to the size of the Himalayan Mountains. But my faith was always in God, the Creator and Source of all that is. It wasn't until recently that I was able to conceive the idea of having faith in man, my fellow brother. And God wants me to start with my husband, Courage. Lord, I trust Courage because I trust You. And so it is!

Seven Tips to Develop Courage

1. Be honest, be open, and live authentically.
2. Be willing to listen and follow the promptings of the Holy Spirit.
3. Honor your passion and commit to action.
4. Try something new and experiment outside your comfort zone.
5. Learn from your mistakes.
6. Believe in yourself.
7. Apply the principles of *The 7 Spiritual Lessons of Relationships* in your significant relationships.

SUGGESTED READING

To Promote Spiritual Growth and Personal Development

Forgiveness

Bourbeau, Lise, *Your Body's Telling You: Love Yourself!*, Les Editions E.T.C. Inc. 2001

Ferrini, Paul, *The Silence of the Heart*, Heartways Press 1996

Muller, Wayne, *Legacy of the Heart*, Simon & Schuster 2002

Tipping, Colin, *Radical Forgiveness*, Sounds True, Inc. 2009

Passion

Burton, Valorie, *Successful Women Think Differently*, Harvest House Publishers 2012

Canfield, Jack, *The Success Principles*, (10th Anniversary Edition), HarperCollins 2015

Hill, Napoleon, *Think and Grow Rich*, The Random House Publishing Group 1960

McMeekin, Gail, *The 12 Secrets of Highly Creative Women*, Conari Press 2000

Seale, Alan, *Soul Mission, Life Vision*, Red Wheel/Weise, LLC 2003

Unconditional Love

Ferrini, Paul, *Love Without Conditions*, Heartways Press 2003

Gawain, Shakti, *The Four Levels of Healing*, Nataraj Publishing 1997

Hendricks, Gay, Ph.D. and Hendricks, Kathlyn, Ph.D., *Conscious Loving: The Journey to Co-Commitment*, Bantam Books 1990

Vanzant, Iyanla, *Living Through the Meantime*, Simon & Schuster 2001

Vanzant, Iyanla, *Until Today!*, Simon & Schuster 2000

Honesty

Owens, Celeste Ph.D., *The 40-Day Surrender Fast*, Good Success Publishing 2011

Tracy, Brian, *No Excuses!*, Da Capo Press 2010

Williams, Terrie M., *Black Pain*, Simon & Schuster, Inc. 2008

Vanzant, Iyanla, *One Day My Soul Just Opened Up*, Simon & Schuster 1998

Vanzant, Iyanla, *The Value in the Valley*, Simon & Schuster 1995

Trust

Butterworth, Eric, *The Universe is Calling*, HarperCollins 1993

Price, John Randolph, *The Angels Within Us*, Ballantine Books 1993

Price, John Randolph, *Practical Spirituality*, Hay House, Inc. 1985

Roman, Sanaya, *Personal Power through Awareness*, H J Kramer Inc. 1986

Faith

Bottorff, J. Douglas, *A Practical Guide to Meditation and Prayer*, Unity 1990

Miller, D. Patrick, *The Book of Practical Faith*, Fearless Books 1999

Muller, Wayne, *Learning to Pray*, Bantam Dell 2003

Harris Smith, Laura, *The 30-Day Faith Detox*, Chosen Books 2016

Courage

Cole, Harriette, *Choosing Truth*, Simon & Schuster 2003

Franklin, DeVon, *The Hollywood Commandments*, HarperCollins 2017

Hill, Napoleon, *The Law of Success*, Penguin Group 2008

McKenna, Paul, *Change Your Life in 7 Days*, Sterling 2010

Meyer, Joyce, *The Confident Woman*, FaithWords 2006

Omartian, Stormie, *The Power of a Praying Wife*, Harvest House Publishers 2014

ABOUT THE AUTHOR

ArDenay Garner is a licensed Master Social Worker and Certified Professional Coach; owner of ArDenay Innerprize, LLC; and founder of The Campaign 42 National Scholarship Foundation. She provides coaching, speaking, and consulting services for aspiring entrepreneurs and small business owners. She has hosted numerous events including her signature LOVE Campaigns, award ceremonies, and various seminars and workshops.

ArDenay received a master's degree in Social Work from Syracuse University in 2014 and bachelor's degree in Business Administration from Columbia College in 2008. In 2010 she completed a two-year personal development program at Inner Visions Institute for Spiritual Development and became a Certified Professional Coach through Fowler Wainwright International. ArDenay is the recipient of the 2006 YWCA Academy of Diversity Achievers Award, and a graduate of the Leadership Greater Syracuse Class of 2007. ArDenay has received a host of other accolades and recognition throughout her career.

ArDenay is committed to helping 79,000 women identify their passion, develop their faith, and pursue entrepreneurship on their own terms with her first book, *Divine Invitations – The 7 Spiritual Lessons of Relationships*. This book is a testament to the trials and tribulations that God delivered her through as a single-parent, survivor of domestic violence, and entrepreneur. She holds steadfast to her faith and purpose-driven mission to be an encourager to everyone in whom she comes in contact.

ArDenay declares that a divine invitation is presented when God gives you the opportunity to transform your pain and suffering into compassion and meaningful work that promotes healing. She uses *Divine Invitations – The 7 Spiritual Lessons of Relationships* to teach women how to practice the spiritual principles of forgiveness, passion, unconditional love, honesty, trust, faith, and courage to move through the daily challenges of intimacy. Using inspirational testimony from her life and specific strategies for spiritual and personal growth, ArDenay will show you how to take responsibility for your feelings and LEAD:

Let go of hurtful memories from the past;

Express compassion for yourself and others;

Awaken your inner creativity and entrepreneurial spirit; and

Discover lessons in self-betrayal that are counterproductive to the life you desire.

Share your thoughts or personal story of trial and triumph with ArDenay!

Email: author@ArDenayGarner.com

Facebook: www.facebook.com/ArDenayGarner

Instagram / Twitter: @ArDenayGarner

Website: www.ArDenayGarner.com

www.ingramcontent.com/pod-product-compliance
Lightning Source LLC
LaVergne TN
LVHW011325080426
835513LV00006B/205